The Ultimate ROUTE 66 COOKBOOK

NORTHLAND
PUBLISHING

The Publisher would like to offer a special thank you
to all of the people across Route 66 who opened up their kitchens
and businesses in order to share their favorite recipes.
We couldn't have completed this book without you!

Photography © 2004
Kerrick James: front cover (top left)
Jim Ross: i
John Running: front cover (bottom right)
David H. Smith: front cover (top right)
Daniel Wend/wendimages.com, classic car images:
iii, 6, 10, 20, 28, 34, 39, 49, 62, 81, 91, 97, 102, 105, back cover
Courtesy of Corbis/Royalty-free stock: iv, 16, 42, 72, 82
Courtesy of Library of Congress, Prints and Photographs Division, photography by
John Vachon: back cover
Courtesy of Metro Diner: front cover (bottom left)
All rights reserved.

www.northlandbooks.com

Composed in the United States of America
Printed in China

Edited by Tammy Gales
Designed by Katie Jennings
Production supervised by Donna Boyd
Index compiled by Jan Williams, Indexing Services

FIRST IMPRESSION 2004
ISBN 10: 0-87358-853-3
ISBN 13: 978-0-87358-853-9

Library of Congress Cataloging-in-Publication Data:
The ultimate Route 66 cookbook.
p.cm.
Includes index.
ISBN 0-87358-853-3 (pbk.)
1. Cookery, American. 2. United States Highway 66.

TX715.U44 2004
641.5973—dc22
2004049560

Contents

Get Your Kicks On ROUTE 66!

Rise & Shine

Wake up to these delicious offerings from kitchens all across historic Route 66.
Add a steaming hot fresh cup of coffee, the morning news,
and you'll be on your way to a perfect day.

MAPLE APPLE NUT MUFFINS
GOLDEN PEACH MUFFINS
CRANBERRY ORANGE SCONES
SOUR CREAM COFFEE CAKE
PLUM QUICK BREAD
DATE PECAN BREAKFAST BREAD
EASY OVERNIGHT CARAMEL ROLLS
EASY OVERNIGHT SAUSAGE ROLLS
MAMAW RUTH'S ROADTRIP BISCUITS
QUICHE LORRAINE
GREEN CHILE QUICHE
BREAKFAST CASSEROLE
TIMBERLINE PANCAKES

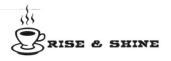
Maple Apple Nut Muffins

DEBBY FUNK, Funks Grove Pure Maple Sirup
Funks Grove, Illinois, (309) 874-3360, www.route66.com/FunksGrove

1 CUP ROLLED OATS
1 CUP BAKING APPLES, COARSELY GRATED
2/3 CUP PURE MAPLE "SIRUP" (THIS IS OUR REAL MAPLE SYRUP.)
1/2 CUP PLAIN YOGURT
1 EGG, BEATEN
1 TEASPOON VANILLA
2 TABLESPOONS VEGETABLE OR OLIVE OIL
1 1/4 CUPS UNBLEACHED FLOUR
2 1/2 TEASPOONS BAKING POWDER
1 1/2 TEASPOONS BAKING SODA
1/2 TEASPOON SALT
1 TEASPOON CINNAMON
1/3 CUP PECANS OR WALNUTS, CHOPPED

Preheat the oven to 400° F. In a **MIXING BOWL**, combine the oats, apples, maple sirup, yogurt, egg, vanilla, and oil. In a **SEPARATE BOWL**, combine the dry ingredients and the nuts and stir into the liquid ingredients. Mix well.

Spoon the batter into 12 large paper-lined **MUFFIN TINS**. Bake for about 15 minutes, or until the tops are springy to touch. Let the muffins cool on a **WIRE RACK** before serving.

It seems wonderful to many people who travel down Route 66 that there is a beautiful stand of hardwood trees consisting predominantly of sugar maples right here in the heart of Illinois.

Route 66 drew part of its lifeblood from this area, as this very farm and its timber have made way for travelers for nearly one hundred years. It first began when Isaac Funk gave land to the railroad. Then, timber was cut to make way for Route 4, which became Route 66 in 1926. In 1953, more farmland and timber were given up to upgrade Route 66 to four lanes. In the early 1970s, another 56 acres were gobbled up when interstate 55 was built to replace 66.

Maybe it is this giving of our soil that has made Route 66 so precious to us. When Isaac Funk settled here in 1822 and founded Funks Grove, he probably never dreamed that it would become known to Route 66 travelers from all over the world or that his great, great, great grandson would be making sirup from the very same trees that he and other early settlers tapped. Funks Grove is a true historic icon of the road.

Golden Peach Muffins

FROM THE KITCHEN OF MARILYN SEUMPTEWA

1 1/2 CUPS ALL-PURPOSE FLOUR
1 CUP SUGAR
3/4 TEASPOON SALT
1/2 TEASPOON BAKING SODA
1/8 TEASPOON GROUND CINNAMON
2 EGGS
1/2 CUP VEGETABLE OIL
1/2 TEASPOON VANILLA EXTRACT
1 (15 1/2-OUNCE) CAN SLICED PEACHES,
    DRAINED AND FINELY CHOPPED

In a **BOWL**, combine the dry ingredients. In another **BOWL**, combine the eggs, oil, and vanilla. Stir the egg mixture into dry ingredients just until moistened (the batter will be thick). Gently fold in the peaches.

Preheat oven to 350° F. Fill paper-lined **MUFFIN CUPS** two-thirds full. Bake for 25-30 minutes, or until a toothpick inserted in the middle comes out clean. Cool for 5 minutes before removing from the pan. Serve warm.

Cranberry Orange Scones

FROM THE KITCHEN OF MARILYN SEUMPTEWA

2 CUPS ALL-PURPOSE FLOUR
10 TEASPOONS SUGAR
1 TABLESPOON GRATED ORANGE PEEL
2 TEASPOONS BAKING POWDER
1/2 TEASPOON SALT
1/4 TEASPOON BAKING SODA
1/3 CUP COLD BUTTER OR MARGARINE
1 CUP DRIED CRANBERRIES
1/4 CUP ORANGE JUICE
1/4 CUP HALF & HALF
1 EGG
1 TABLESPOON MILK

GLAZE:
1/2 CUP CONFECTIONER'S SUGAR
1 TABLESPOON ORANGE JUICE

ORANGE BUTTER:
1/2 CUP BUTTER, SOFTENED
2-3 TABLESPOONS ORANGE MARMALADE

Preheat oven to 400° F. In a **MEDIUM BOWL**, combine the flour, 7 teaspoons of the sugar, the orange peel, baking powder, salt, and baking soda. Cut in the butter until the mixture resembles coarse crumbs; set aside. In a **SMALL BOWL**, combine the cranberries, orange juice, half and half, and the egg. Add to the flour mixture and stir until a soft dough forms. On a floured surface, gently knead 6-8 times. Pat the dough into an 8-inch circle. Cut into 10 wedges. Separate the wedges and place on an ungreased **BAKING SHEET**. Brush lightly with milk, and sprinkle with the remaining sugar. Bake for 12-15 minutes, or until lightly browned. Remove from the oven and allow to cool slightly.

In a **SMALL BOWL**, combine the glaze ingredients and drizzle over the warm scones. In a **SEPARATE BOWL**, combine the orange butter ingredients. Pour into a **DECORATIVE SERVING BOWL**, and serve on the side with the warm scones.

Sour Cream Coffee Cake

FROM THE KITCHEN OF CAROLE HORTON

1 STICK BUTTER
1 CUP SUGAR
2 EGGS
1 TEASPOON VANILLA
2 CUPS ALL-PURPOSE FLOUR
1 TEASPOON BAKING POWDER
1 TEASPOON BAKING SODA
1/2 TEASPOON SALT
1/2 PINT SOUR CREAM

TOPPING:
1/2 CUP SUGAR
1 TEASPOON CINNAMON

Preheat the oven to 350° F. In **LARGE BOWL**, mix the butter, sugar, eggs, and vanilla. In a separate **SMALL BOWL**, mix the flour, baking powder, baking soda, and the salt. Add the dry mixture to the large bowl of the butter mixture. Mix in the sour cream.

To make the topping, mix the sugar and the cinnamon. Set aside. Grease a **TUBE PAN** and pour half of the cake batter into it. Sprinkle the top with half of the topping mixture. Add the rest of the batter, and then top with the remaining topping mixture. Bake for 40 minutes or until set. When the cake is done, remove from the oven and cover the pan with a loose sheet of aluminum foil. Keep the cake covered until cool. Slice and serve with a hot cup of coffee.

Plum Quick Bread

FROM THE KITCHEN OF MARILYN SEUMPTEWA

3 EGGS
2 (6-OUNCE) JARS PLUM BABY FOOD
1 CUP VEGETABLE OIL
1 CUP BUTTERMILK
2 1/2 CUPS ALL-PURPOSE FLOUR
2 CUPS SUGAR
2 TEASPOONS BAKING SODA
1 TEASPOON GROUND CINNAMON
1/2 TEASPOON SALT

Preheat the oven to 350° F. In a **MIXING BOWL**, combine the eggs, baby food, oil, and buttermilk. In a **SEPARATE BOWL**, combine the dry ingredients. Add to the egg mixture and beat just until moistened. Transfer to two greased **9X5X3-INCH LOAF PANS**.

Bake for 60-65 minutes, or until a toothpick inserted near the center comes out clean. Cool for 10 minutes before removing from the pans. Serve warm.

Date Pecan Breakfast Bread

FROM THE KITCHEN OF MARILYN SEUMPTEWA

2 1/2 CUPS DATES, CHOPPED
1 1/2 CUPS BOILING WATER
1 1/2 TEASPOONS BAKING SODA
1 3/4 CUPS ALL-PURPOSE FLOUR
1 1/4 TEASPOONS GROUND CLOVES
1 1/4 TEASPOONS CINNAMON
1 1/4 TEASPOONS GINGER
1 1/4 TEASPOONS NUTMEG
2 TABLESPOONS BUTTER OR
    MARGARINE, SOFTENED
1 1/4 CUPS SUGAR
1 EGG
2 TEASPOONS VANILLA EXTRACT
1 1/2 CUPS PECANS, COARSELY CHOPPED

Preheat the oven to 350° F. Place the dates in a **MEDIUM BOWL**. In
a separate **SMALL BOWL**, combine the boiling water and baking soda.
Pour over the dates. In **ANOTHER BOWL**, combine the flour, cloves,
cinnamon, ginger, and nutmeg; set aside.

   In a **MIXING BOWL**, cream the softened butter and sugar. Beat in
the egg and vanilla. Add the dry ingredients alternately with the date
mixture. Stir in the pecans. Pour into a greased and floured **9X5X3-
INCH LOAF PAN**. Bake 65-75 minutes, or until a toothpick inserted near
the center comes out clean. Cool for 10 minutes before removing from
the pan. Allow to completely cool on a **WIRE RACK** before serving.

Easy Overnight Caramel Rolls

SHARON STEVENS, Stevens Farm Inn
5484 Hwy OO, Marshfield, MO 65706, (417) 859-6525, www.usipp.com/stevensfarm

1 DOZEN FROZEN ROLLS
1 PACKAGE BUTTERSCOTCH PUDDING MIX
   (THE KIND YOU COOK)
1 CUP BROWN SUGAR
1/2 CUP BUTTER OR MARGARINE, MELTED
1/3 CUP PECANS, COARSELY CHOPPED

Spray a **BUNT PAN** or an **ANGEL FOOD CAKE PAN** with nonstick cooking spray. Place the rolls in the pan, sprinkle the whole package of butterscotch pudding mix over the rolls, sprinkle the brown sugar over the pudding mix, pour the margarine over the sugar, and top with the pecans. Cover and place in the refrigerator overnight, or let rise for 4-5 hours before baking.

Preheat the oven to 350° F. Bake the rolls for 20-25 minutes. Let cool, and then place them on a **DECORATIVE SERVING PLATE**.

Stevens Farm is a horse motel and overnight facility for both horses and their riders. We have easy access from MO I-44, and as everyone knows, it's a good thing to be able to stay with your horse when traveling! Stevens Farm raises Champion Paint and Quarter horses, and we usually always have foals and horses for sale. Contact us at www.Route66.com or at www.Horsemotel.com.

Easy Overnight Sausage Rolls

SHARON STEVENS, Stevens Farm Inn
5484 Hwy OO, Marshfield, MO 65706, (417) 859-6525, www.usipp.com/stevensfarm

**2 PACKAGES FROZEN WHITE BREAD
DOUGH, THAWED
1 1/2 POUNDS SAUSAGE
1 GREEN PEPPER, CHOPPED
1 MEDIUM ONION, CHOPPED
1 CUP AMERICAN CHEESE, SHREDDED**

Roll out each package of bread dough so that it is big enough to fill with sausage mixture. In a **MEDIUM PAN**, cook the sausage with the green peppers and onions. Drain excess liquid. Spread half of the sausage mixture on each rolled out piece of dough, and sprinkle each with 1/2 cup of the cheese. Roll up each piece of dough so that it completely covers the sausage and cheese mixture. Cover and let raise overnight in the refrigerator, or for 4-5 hours before baking.

Preheat the oven to 350° F. Bake the rolls for 20-25 minutes, and then brush lightly with butter. Cover the rolls while they cool so that they soften up, and then slice and serve warm.

Mamaw Ruth's Roadtrip Biscuits

FROM THE KITCHEN OF ERIC HOWARD

1 PACKAGE RAPID RISE YEAST
1 TEASPOON SUGAR
1/2 CUP WARM WATER
3 CUPS ALL-PURPOSE FLOUR
2 TABLESPOONS SUGAR
1 TEASPOON BAKING POWDER
3/4 TEASPOON SALT
1/4 TEASPOON BAKING SODA
1/4 CUP OIL
1 CUP BUTTERMILK

Preheat the oven to 450° F. In a **SMALL BOWL**, mix together the yeast, 1 teaspoon of the sugar, and the water. Set aside. In a **SEPARATE BOWL**, mix together the dry ingredients. Make a well in the middle and add the yeast mixture, the oil, and the buttermilk. Stir the dry ingredients into the wet ingredients until the mixture holds together. Remove the dough from the bowl, place on a floured **BOARD**, and knead a few times. Pat out to desired the thickness, about 1/4-inch thick, and then cut into squares with a floured knife or into circles with a greased cookie cutter.

   Add approximately 2 tablespoons of oil to the bottom of an **OVEN-PROOF SKILLET** and spread it around to coat the bottom. Place the biscuits in the skillet, turning over once to coat with oil. Cover and let rise for about 45 minutes. Once the biscuits have risen, place the skillet in the oven and bake until brown, approximately 15 minutes. Serve with eggs and sausage or alone as a nice, hearty breakfast. Good eating!

Quiche Lorraine

FROM THE KITCHEN OF SUE SCHNAPP

1 PRE-BAKED 9-INCH PIE SHELL
10 SLICES BACON, FRIED CRISP AND CRUMBLED
1 CUP SWISS CHEESE, GRATED
2 CUPS HALF & HALF
4 EGGS, WELL BEATEN
3/4 TEASPOON SALT
BLACK PEPPER, TO TASTE
1/2 TEASPOON SUGAR
1/2 CUP MUSHROOMS, SLICED

Preheat the oven to 350° F. If desired, lightly butter the pie shell. Sprinkle the crumbled bacon on the bottom of the shell, and then add the cheese. In a **SEPARATE BOWL**, combine the remaining ingredients. Pour the egg mixture into the **PIE SHELL**. Bake for 30 minutes, or until a knife inserted in the center comes out clean. Serve warm.

RISE & SHINE

Green Chile Quiche

FROM THE KITCHEN OF MARILYN SEUMPTEWA

1 UNBAKED 9-INCH PASTRY SHELL
1 ¹/₂ CUPS HALF & HALF
4 EGGS
SALT, TO TASTE
BLACK PEPPER, TO TASTE
2 CUPS SWISS CHEESE, SHREDDED
2 TABLESPOONS ALL-PURPOSE FLOUR
8 SLICES BACON, COOKED AND CRUMBLED
1 CUP CHICKEN, COOKED AND SHREDDED
2-3 ROASTED GREEN CHILES, CHOPPED

Preheat the oven to 350° F. In a **MEDIUM BOWL**, combine the half and half, eggs, salt, and pepper. Mix well. In a **SEPARATE BOWL**, toss the cheese and flour, and then add to the egg mixture. Add the bacon, chicken, and chiles. Pour into the shell. Bake for 40-45 minutes, or until a knife inserted in the center comes out clean. Allow to cool slightly, and then serve warm.

Breakfast Casserole

FROM THE KITCHEN OF TUNIE HIEHLE

1 1/2 POUNDS SAUSAGE

9 EGGS, SLIGHTLY BEATEN

3 CUPS MILK

1 1/2 TEASPOONS DRY MUSTARD

1 TEASPOON SALT

3 SLICES BREAD WITH THE CRUSTS REMOVED, CUT INTO 12 PIECES

1 1/2 CUPS CHEDDAR CHEESE, SHREDDED

Brown the sausage, and then drain excess liquid. In a **MEDIUM BOWL**, mix the eggs, milk, dry mustard, and salt. Stir in the bread pieces, cheese, and sausage. Pour the mixture into a **9X13-INCH GREASED PAN**. Arrange the bread so it is evenly spaced. Cover and refrigerate overnight.

About 1 hour before you are ready to serve the casserole, preheat the oven to 350° F. Bake, uncovered, for approximately 1 hour, or until the casserole is set. Serve warm.

Timberline Pancakes

DAVID KNUDSON, EXECUTIVE DIRECTOR, National Historic Route 66 Federation
P.O. Box 1848, Lake Arrowhead, CA 92352, (909) 336-6131, www.national66.org

**1 BOX KRUSTEAZ BUTTERMILK PANCAKE MIX
   (IT MUST BE THIS BRAND)
¹/4 TEASPOON NUTMEG
¹/4 TEASPOON CINNAMON
¹/4 TEASPOON VANILLA
1 TEASPOON SUGAR
1 CUP FRESH BLUEBERRIES, OR 1 CUP BANANAS,
   THINLY SLICED**

Mix the pancake batter as directed on the box. (The directions will
ask you to add water to the mix. Adhere to this and never add milk or
eggs.) Add slightly more water to the mixed batter so that it is runny
and lumpy. Stir in the nutmeg, cinnamon, vanilla, and sugar. Add more
depending on your tastes.

Coat the bottom of a griddle with a little oil and approximately 1
tablespoon of butter. Allow the **GRIDDLE** to heat up enough so that
the butter has completely melted. Pour out enough pancakes to fill
the griddle, and immediately add the blueberries or bananas, making
sure to carefully push them into each pancake. Do not try to mix them
up in the batter, as this will create a mess. Fry the pancakes, turning
once, until golden brown. Serve immediately.

These are guaranteed to be the best pancakes you've ever eaten.

The History of the Federation

Over 40 years ago, David Knudson drove from Chicago to California on Route 66. Fresh out of college, he had pocket change, plenty of dreams, and no job. He stayed and eventually built a business in Los Angeles. But, he never forgot his trip across Route 66 with all the fancy motor courts, exotic trading posts, and the aroma of sweet smoke from the pit barbecues. He couldn't afford to stop at any of them, but he vowed one day that he'd travel down Route 66 again and buy some moccasins, sample the great-smelling barbecue, and stay in a few places with clean sheets.

In August of 1994, his chance came. His wife, Mary Lou, and he were in Chicago and decided to drive back to California. But, they couldn't find Route 66! It wasn't on any maps and the "66" road signs were long gone. The old road had been bypassed by an interstate over 20 years earlier, stranding many of the once-thriving businesses and towns. Their deserted structures stood only as silent reminders of the days of "America's Glory Road."

By the time David and Mary Lou arrived home, they decided to sell their business interests and devote their time to trying to save as much as possible of the historic road before it was completely gone. With that, the Federation was born.

The Federation has just moved into new and larger quarters in The San Bernardino Mountains overlooking Route 66.

The Mission and Goals of the Federation

The National Historic Route 66 Federation is the worldwide, nonprofit organization dedicated to directing the public's attention to the importance of Route 66 in America's cultural heritage; acquiring the federal, state, and private support necessary to preserve the historic landmarks; and revitalizing the economies of communities along the entire 2,400-mile stretch of road. The Federation accomplishes these goals through public education, advocacy, and membership activities. Public outreach strategies include publication of the quarterly magazine Federation News; the Adopt-A-Hundred Preservation Program; the presentation of the John Steinbeck Award to an individual who has made a major difference in the preservation of Route 66, and the Cyrus Avery Award for an outstanding preservation project; a worldwide website; the Route 66 Dining & Lodging Guide; special events and assistance to the media, authors, learning institutions, and production companies.

Munchies & Lite Bites

In this chapter, you will find a wide array of delicious snacks, inventive soups and salads, home-style sandwiches, and fast food for the road. These dishes are also great to serve at family get-togethers and summertime pool parties. Bring out these quick and easy treats, set the Route 66 theme, and watch your guests dive right in!

BAKED SPINACH & ARTICHOKE DIP

PIÑA COLADA FRUIT DIP

APPLE DIP

TOSSED SALAD WITH MAPLE RASPBERRY VINAIGRETTE

PEAR SALAD WITH FETA, BACON, & HAZELNUTS

RAMEN NOODLE CABBAGE SALAD

SWEET SESAME SALAD

GREEK SALAD

ORZO SPINACH SALAD

STRAWBERRY SPINACH SALAD WITH CANDIED PECANS

CREAM OF POTATO SOUP

POSOLE

FIVE BEAN SOUP

BUTTERNUT SQUASH & APPLE SOUP

JAMBALAYA

ARTICHOKE MELTS

SPINACH & FETA CHEESE FRITTATA

TOSTADA LUNCHEON QUICHE

VEGGIE QUESADILLAS

CHICKEN & HAM ROLL-UPS

HOT CHICKEN SALAD IN A RING

SWEET & SOUR MEATBALLS

SPICY MEATBALLS

HOMEMADE SLOPPY JOES

VEGETARIAN "MEAT" SANDWICHES

Baked Spinach & Artichoke Dip

FROM THE KITCHEN OF KAREN BILLIDEAU

**1 (10-OUNCE) PACKAGE FROZEN SPINACH,
    THAWED, SQUEEZED DRY, AND CHOPPED
1 (14-OUNCE) CAN ARTICHOKE HEARTS,
    DRAINED AND CHOPPED
1/2 CUP PARMESAN CHEESE, GRATED
1 CUP MOZZARELLA CHEESE, SHREDDED
1/4 TEASPOON GROUND WHITE PEPPER
1 POUND CREAM CHEESE, SOFTENED
2 CLOVES GARLIC, MINCED**

Preheat oven to 350° F. In a **MEDIUM BOWL**, combine all ingredients. Mix well, and spoon mixture into a **1 QUART BAKING DISH** sprayed with nonstick cooking spray.

Bake for 15-20 minutes, or until hot and bubbly. Place in a **DECORATIVE SERVING BOWL**, and serve with crackers or tortilla chips.

Piña Colada Fruit Dip

FROM THE KITCHEN OF MARY GALES

**1 (8-OUNCE) CAN CRUSHED PINEAPPLE
IN ITS OWN JUICE, UNDRAINED
1 (3 ½-OUNCE) PACKAGE INSTANT
COCONUT PUDDING
½ CUP MILK
½ CUP DAIRY SOUR CREAM**

In a **LARGE BOWL**, mix all ingredients. Place in a **FOOD PROCESSOR**
or **BLENDER**, cover, and blend for 30 seconds. Return to the bowl
and refrigerate for at least 3 hours so that the flavors can blend. Place
in a **DECORATIVE SERVING BOWL**, and serve with as assortment of
fresh fruit.

Apple Dip

FROM THE KITCHEN OF SANDY RACEK

**8 OUNCES SOFT CREAM CHEESE
½ CUP WHITE SUGAR
¼ CUP BROWN SUGAR
1 TEASPOON VANILLA**

Place all ingredients in a **MEDIUM-SIZE BOWL**, and beat until soft
and smooth. Place in a **SERVING BOWL** and surround with apple
slices. Serve immediately.

Tossed Salad with Maple Raspberry Vinaigrette

DEBBY FUNK, Funks Grove Pure Maple Sirup
Funks Grove, Illinois, (309) 874-3360, www.route66.com/FunksGrove

SALAD:
1 HEAD LETTUCE, COARSELY CHOPPED
2 CARROTS, CHOPPED
1 ONION, THINLY SLICED
3 ROMA TOMATOES, CHOPPED

VINAIGRETTE:
1/4 CUP RASPBERRY VINEGAR
1/2 CUP EXTRA LIGHT OLIVE OIL
1/4 CUP PURE MAPLE "SIRUP"
2 TEASPOON SPICY BROWN MUSTARD
2 TEASPOON CRUMBLED TARRAGON LEAVES

In a **LARGE BOWL**, combine the lettuce, carrots, onion slices, and tomatoes. Add any other salad ingredients you desire. Set aside. In a **SMALL SEPARATE BOWL**, combine all of the vinaigrette ingredients and mix well. Pour over the tossed salad and mix so that the whole salad is well coated. Serve in individual bowls. This vinaigrette is a delicious addition to any side salad.

Pear Salad with Feta, Bacon, Hazelnuts, & Shallot Vinaigrette

FROM THE KITCHEN OF ROBIN WRIGHT

1 TABLESPOON PLUS 1/2 CUP OLIVE OIL
3/4 CUP SHALLOTS, THINLY SLICED
8 BACON SLICES
5 TABLESPOONS SHERRY WINE VINEGAR
SALT, TO TASTE
BLACK PEPPER, TO TASTE
8 CUPS WATERCRESS (ABOUT 2 LARGE BUNCHES), LOOSELY PACKED AND TRIMMED
2 HEADS BELGIAN ENDIVE, TRIMMED AND SLICED CROSSWISE
3 RIPE PEARS, HALVED, CORED, AND THINLY SLICED
3/4 CUP FETA CHEESE, CRUMBLED
1/3 CUP HUSKED TOASTED HAZELNUTS, COARSELY CHOPPED

Heat 1 tablespoon oil in **LARGE NONSTICK SKILLET** over medium heat. Add the shallots and sauté until tender and golden, about 8 minutes. Transfer the shallots to a **SMALL BOWL** and let cool. Cook the bacon in the same skillet until crisp. Transfer the bacon to paper towels and drain. Crumble the bacon into small pieces and set aside.

In a **MEDIUM BOWL**, mix the vinegar and remaining 1/2 cup of oil. Stir in the sautéed shallots and season the mixture generously with salt and pepper.

In a **SALAD BOWL**, combine the watercress, endive, and pears. Pour the vinegar dressing over salad and toss to coat. Sprinkle with feta cheese, hazelnuts, and bacon. Serve immediately.

Ramen Noodle Cabbage Salad

FROM THE KITCHEN OF MERRY ANNE ROSENGREN

DRESSING:
3 TABLESPOONS SUGAR
2 TABLESPOONS VINEGAR
1/2 CUP OIL
1 PACKET BEEF SPICE (FROM THE RAMEN)

SALAD:
1 HEAD CABBAGE, CHOPPED
1/2 ONION, CHOPPED
3 TABLESPOONS SESAME SEEDS, LIGHTLY TOASTED
1/2 CUP SLIVERED ALMONDS, LIGHTLY TOASTED
1 PACKAGE RAMEN NOODLES, CRUSHED

Mix the dressing ingredients and chill in the refrigerator while making the salad. In a **LARGE BOWL**, mix together the salad ingredients. Add the dressing and toss well so that the entire salad is coated. Serve immediately.

Sweet Sesame Salad

FROM THE KITCHEN OF MARILYN SEUMPTEWA

1 (10-OUNCE) PACKAGE MIXED SALAD GREENS
1 MEDIUM TOMATO, CUT INTO THIN WEDGES
2/3 CUP BALSAMIC VINAIGRETTE PREPARED SALAD DRESSING
2 TEASPOONS HONEY
1 (11-OUNCE) CAN MANDARIN ORANGES, DRAINED
1 TEASPOON SESAME SEEDS, TOASTED

In a **LARGE SALAD BOWL**, combine the greens and the tomato wedges. Set aside. In a **JAR** with a tight lid, combine the salad dressing and the honey. Cover and shake well. Drizzle over the salad and toss to coat. Sprinkle the top with oranges and sesame seeds. Serve with a side of fresh bread.

Greek Salad

FROM THE KITCHEN OF KAREN BILLIDEAU

1 HEAD ROMAINE LETTUCE, TORN INTO BITE-SIZED PIECES
3 VINE-RIPENED TOMATOES, CUT INTO CHUNKS
1 RED ONION, THINLY SLICED
1/2 SEEDLESS CUCUMBER, CUT INTO BITE-SIZE CHUNKS
5 RADISHES, SLICED
1 CUP KALAMATA OLIVES, PITTED
1/2 POUND FETA CHEESE, CRUMBLED
1/4 CUP OLIVE OIL
3 LEMONS, JUICED
3 CLOVES GARLIC, CRUSHED
1 TEASPOON DRIED OREGANO, CRUSHED
COARSE SALT, TO TASTE
BLACK PEPPER, TO TASTE

In a **LARGE SERVING BOWL**, combine the lettuce, tomatoes, onion, cucumber, radishes, olives, and crumbled feta cheese. In a separate **SMALL CONTAINER** that has a lid, mix the oil, lemon juice, garlic, and oregano. Cover and shake vigorously. Pour generously over the salad and toss to coat well. Season with salt and pepper and let the salad marinate until ready to serve. Serve with fresh, warm pita bread.

Orzo Spinach Salad

THE ADAM FAMILY, The Ariston Café
South Old Route 66, Litchfield, IL 62056, (217) 324-2023, www.ariston-cafe.com

1 POUND ORZO
¹/₂ POUND FROZEN SPINACH
1 CUP KALAMATA OLIVES, PITTED
    AND CUT IN HALF
1 ¹/₂ CUPS FETA CHEESE, CRUMBLED
1 SMALL RED ONION, CHOPPED
¹/₂ STALK CELERY, CHOPPED
¹/₂ CUP OLIVE OIL
¹/₄ CUP BALSAMIC VINEGAR
1 TABLESPOON GARLIC POWDER
¹/₂ TEASPOON SALT
1 TEASPOON WHITE PEPPER

In a **MEDIUM POT**, boil the orzo and drain. Set aside. Blanch the
frozen spinach and drain well. In a **LARGE SERVING BOWL**, mix all of
the remaining ingredients together with the orzo and cooked spinach.
Serve immediately. This orzo-spinach salad is one of our favorites!

*The Ariston Café has been open since 1924, first in Carlinville, and
then in Litchfield in 1929. The Ariston moved to its present location in
Litchfield in 1935, and it is still serving locals and weary travelers of
Route 66 and Illinois 16. The Café has always been owned by the
Adam Family.*

Strawberry Spinach Salad with Candied Pecans

FROM THE KITCHEN OF ROBIN WRIGHT

DRESSING:
2/3 CUP WHITE VINEGAR
1/2 CUP SUGAR
3 GREEN ONIONS, CHOPPED
1 1/2 TEASPOONS SALT
2 TEASPOONS DRY MUSTARD
2 CUPS VEGETABLE OIL
3 TABLESPOONS POPPY SEEDS

SALAD:
2 TABLESPOONS BUTTER OR MARGARINE
1 1/2 CUPS PECAN HALVES
1 CUP SUGAR
1 POUND FRESH SPINACH
2 CUPS CELERY, THINLY SLICED
1 PINT FRESH STRAWBERRIES, HALVED

In an electric **BLENDER**, combine all of the dressing ingredients
except for the oil and poppy seeds. Cover and process until smooth.
While the blender is still running, gradually add the oil. Process until
thick and smooth. Transfer the dressing to a **BOWL** and stir in the
poppy seeds. Cover and chill.

Melt the butter in a **LARGE HEAVY SKILLET** over medium heat.
Add pecans and sugar. Stir to combine. Cook, stirring constantly, until
the sugar melts around the pecans and is caramel-colored. Remove
the pecans with a slotted spoon and spread in a single layer on a
sheet of lightly greased aluminum foil. Cool completely and break into
bite-sized pieces. Set aside.

Wash the spinach and pat dry with paper towels. In a **LARGE
BOWL**, mix the spinach, celery, and strawberries. Pour 1 cup of the
dressing over the salad and toss gently. Add the reserved candied
pecans. Serve immediately with remaining dressing on the side.

Cream of Potato Soup

FROM THE KITCHEN OF MARY GALES

1 (16-OUNCE) CAN CHICKEN BROTH (USE THE LOW SALT VARIETY)
3 CUPS POTATOES, CUBED
1/4 CUP FLOUR
2 CUPS MILK
1/8 TEASPOON PEPPER
2 LARGE CARROTS, PEELED AND CUT INTO THIN STRIPS
1/2 CUP CHEDDAR CHEESE, FINELY SHREDDED

Place the chicken broth in a **LARGE SOUP POT** and bring to a boil. Add the potatoes and turn heat to medium. Continue to cook the potatoes over medium heat for 10 minutes, or until they are soft, stirring occasionally.

In **SMALL BOWL**, combine the flour, milk, and pepper. Blend until smooth. Slowly stir into the potato mixture. Add the carrots and the cheese and cook until soup is thick. Serve hot.

Posole

LA CITA RESTAURANT
812 South 1st Street, Tucumcari, NM 88401, (505) 461-0949

2 POUNDS CUBED PORK
**1/2 LARGE BAG OR 3 (15-OUNCE) CANS
   HOMINY, DRAINED**
1 GALLON WATER
3 CLOVES GARLIC, CHOPPED
1 TABLESPOON OREGANO
SALT, TO TASTE
BLACK PEPPER, TO TASTE
1 TEASPOON ONION POWDER
1/2 TEASPOON SEASONING SALT
1 TABLESPOON RED CHILI POWDER
1 MEDIUM ONION, COARSELY CHOPPED

Put the pork and hominy in a **STOCK PAN** and add the water. Bring to
a boil. Turn down the heat and simmer for two hours. Then add the
garlic, oregano, salt, pepper, onion powder, seasoning salt, and red
chili powder. Cook until the hominy puffs up, or is tender. Just before
serving, stir in the chopped onion. Spoon into **DECORATIVE SERVING
BOWLS**, and serve warm.

Five Bean Soup

THE ADAM FAMILY, The Ariston Café
South Old Route 66, Litchfield, IL 62056, (217) 324-2023, www.ariston-cafe.com

3 CUPS DRIED KIDNEY BEANS
3 CUPS DRIED LIMA BEANS
3 CUPS DRIED GREAT NORTHERN BEANS
3 CUPS DRIED PINTO BEANS
3 CUPS DRIED SPLIT PEAS
4 (20-OUNCE) CANS TOMATOES, CRUSHED
1 STALK CELERY, CHOPPED
1 GREEN PEPPER, CHOPPED
1 ONION, CHOPPED
2 TABLESPOONS WHITE PEPPER
2 TABLESPOONS CUMIN
2 TABLESPOONS GARLIC POWDER
3 BAY LEAVES
4 CUPS WATER (ADD MORE FOR A THINNER SOUP)

Prepare the dried beans according to the package directions. After beans have soaked overnight, rinse them and place in a **LARGE SOUP POT** with the remaining ingredients. Mix well. Bring to a boil, and then reduce the heat to simmer. Cover and cook until the split peas, celery, and onion are done, approximately 2-3 hours. This is a very popular soup with our customers.

Butternut Squash & Apple Soup

FROM THE KITCHEN OF CATHY LEWIS

3 TABLESPOONS UNSALTED BUTTER
1 ONION, CHOPPED
1 MEDIUM BUTTERNUT SQUASH, PEELED
 AND CUT INTO 1-INCH CUBES
6 CUPS LOW SODIUM CHICKEN BROTH
4 GRANNY SMITH APPLES, PEELED, CORED,
 AND CHOPPED
4 PINCHES OF SPANISH SAFFRON THREADS
1 PINCH NUTMEG, FRESHLY GRATED
2 CUPS HEAVY CREAM
SALT, TO TASTE
FRESHLY GROUND PEPPER, TO TASTE

In a **LARGE SOUP POT**, melt the butter. When the butter has just stopped foaming, add the onion and sauté, stirring occasionally, until tender and translucent, about 4-6 minutes. Add the squash and broth, bring to a boil, and reduce the heat to medium-low. Simmer, stirring occasionally, until the squash is tender when pierced with a fork, about 20 minutes.

Add the apples, saffron, and nutmeg and simmer, stirring occasionally, until the apples are tender, about 15 minutes more. Using a **FOOD PROCESSOR** or **BLENDER**, purée the soup in batches until smooth. Return the soup to the pot, stir in the cream and season with salt and pepper. Warm gently as needed.

Jambalaya

FROM THE KITCHEN OF CATHY LEWIS

2 1/2 CUPS COOKED HAM, CUBED
1/2 POUND COOKED SHRIMP
5 SLICES BACON
1 MEDIUM ONION, MINCED
1 CLOVE GARLIC, MINCED
1 (10-OUNCE) CAN CONDENSED
   CHICKEN BROTH
1 CUP WATER
1 BAY LEAF
1/2 TEASPOON THYME
1 1/2 CUPS REGULAR RICE
1 MEDIUM GREEN PEPPER
1 (16-OUNCE) CAN TOMATOES
1/2 TEASPOON SALT
3-4 DROPS HOT PEPPER SAUCE

In a **LARGE SKILLET** over medium heat, fry the bacon until crisp. Drain on paper towels, crumble, and set aside. In the same skillet over medium heat, cook the rice, onion, green pepper, and garlic until the rice is slightly browned. Stir in the tomatoes and their liquid with the chicken broth, water, bay leaf, salt, and thyme. Cover and simmer for 15 minutes. Stir in the ham, shrimp, and hot sauce. Cover and cook, stirring occasionally, for 15-20 minutes until the rice is tender.

Spoon into **INDIVIDUAL SERVING BOWLS**, sprinkle each with the crumbled bacon, and serve.

Artichoke Melts

FROM THE KITCHEN OF ROBIN WRIGHT

6 SLICES FIRM WHITE BREAD
1 (14-OUNCE) CAN ARTICHOKE HEARTS IN WATER,
**   DRAINED AND CHOPPED**
3/4 CUP FRESH PARMESAN CHEESE, GRATED
1/4 CUP MAYONNAISE
1 CLOVE GARLIC, PRESSED
1 (4-OUNCE) CAN SLICED OLIVES
24 SPRIGS FRESH PARSLEY

Preheat the oven to 350° F. Cut the crusts off of the bread and cut each slice into 4 squares for a total of 24 squares. Place the squares on a **BAKING SHEET**.

In a **SMALL BOWL**, combine the chopped artichokes, 1/2 cup of the grated Parmesan, the mayonnaise, and the pressed garlic. Mix well.

Place one teaspoon of artichoke mixture on each bread square, and sprinkle with remaining Parmesan. Top each with sliced olives and a sprig of parsley. Bake for 25-30 minutes, or until the edges of the bread are golden brown. Remove to a **DECORATIVE PLATTER** and serve warm.

Spinach & Feta Cheese Frittata

FROM THE KITCHEN OF KAREN BILLIDEAU

2 TABLESPOONS OLIVE OIL
1 ONION, FINELY CHOPPED
6 LARGE EGGS, BEATEN
1 POUND SPINACH, STEMS REMOVED,
    WASHED, AND CHOPPED
SALT, TO TASTE
BLACK PEPPER, TO TASTE
¼ CUP FETA CHEESE

In a **9-INCH SKILLET**, heat the olive oil over medium heat. Add the onions and cook, stirring until soft, about 5 minutes.

In a **MIXING BOWL**, combine the eggs, spinach, salt, and pepper. Add the cheese and mix well. Pour this mixture into the skillet and cook until the bottom has set, about 5 minutes. Holding a **FLAT LID** over the skillet, turn the frittata over onto the other side and slide it back into the skillet. Cook for 5 more minutes and serve warm with marinara sauce or salsa.

Tostada Luncheon Quiche

FROM THE KITCHEN OF ROBIN WRIGHT

1 (9-INCH) UNBAKED PASTRY SHELL
8 OUNCES GROUND BEEF
1/4 CUP ONION, CHOPPED
1 (4-OUNCE) CAN DICED GREEN CHILES
1-2 TABLESPOONS TACO SEASONING MIX
1 1/2 CUPS CHEDDAR CHEESE, SHREDDED
3 EGGS, SLIGHTLY BEATEN
1 1/2 CUPS HALF & HALF
1/2 TEASPOON SALT
BLACK PEPPER, TO TASTE

Preheat the oven to 400° F. Bake the pastry shell for approximately 7 minutes. Remove from the oven and set aside. Reduce the temperature to 375° F. In a **MEDIUM SKILLET** combine the ground beef, onion, green chiles, and taco seasoning. Cook until the onions are tender and the meat is brown. Drain the beef mixture. In the pastry shell, layer the cheese and then beef mixture.

In a **MEDIUM MIXING BOWL**, mix the eggs, half & half, salt, and pepper. Pour the egg mixture into the pastry shell over the meat and cheese. Bake for 45 minutes, or until a knife inserted in the center comes out clean. Let stand for 10 minutes before serving.

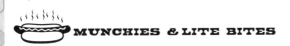
Veggie Quesadillas

FROM THE KITCHEN OF ROBIN WRIGHT

1 CUP ROASTED BELL PEPPER SALSA
1 CUP BLACK BEANS, DRAINED AND RINSED
1 ZUCCHINI, CHOPPED
8 (8-INCH) FLOUR TORTILLAS
3/4 CUP MONTEREY JACK CHEESE, SHREDDED

In a **MEDIUM BOWL**, combine the salsa, beans, and zucchini. Spread 1/4 of the mixture on each of 4 flour tortillas. Top each tortilla with approximately 3 tablespoons of the cheese. Cover each tortilla with one of the remaining tortillas.

Heat a **MEDIUM-SIZED NONSTICK SKILLET** over medium heat. One at a time, carefully cook each quesadilla, turning once, until cheese is melted. Cut each quesadilla into quarters and serve with a side of chips and salsa.

Chicken & Ham Roll-ups

FROM THE KITCHEN OF SUE SCHNAPP

6 BONELESS, SKINLESS CHICKEN BREASTS
6 SLICES BOILED HAM
2 TABLESPOONS BUTTER
1 (16-OUNCE) CAN CREAM OF MUSHROOM SOUP
8 OUNCES SOUR CREAM
¼ CUP WHITE WINE

Preheat the oven to 350° F. Place the chicken between 2 sheets of waxed paper. Using a meat tenderizer, flatten the chicken. Remove from the waxed paper, and top each chicken breast with 1 slice of ham. Roll up the meat and secure with toothpick.

In a **MEDIUM FRYING PAN**, melt the butter. Lightly brown the rolled chicken and ham. Place the roll-ups in an **8X8 PAN**.

In a **SEPARATE BOWL**, stir together the soup, sour cream, and wine. Pour the soup mixture over the chicken roll-ups, and cover the dish with aluminum foil. Bake for 30-40 minutes. These roll-ups are delicious when served with noodles or rice.

Hot Chicken Salad in a Ring

FROM THE KITCHEN OF DALE NEWHART

1 1/2 CUPS CHICKEN, COOKED AND DICED
1 (8-OUNCE) CAN PINEAPPLE CHUNKS, DRAINED
1/2 CUP MAYONNAISE
1/4 CUP RED PEPPER, CHOPPED
1/4 CUP ALMONDS
1/4 CUP GREEN PEPPERS, CHOPPED
1/2 CUP LEEK, SLICED
SALT, TO TASTE
BLACK PEPPER, TO TASTE
1 CAN CRESCENT ROLLS
2 EGGS, BEATEN

Preheat the oven to 350° F. In a **MEDIUM BOWL**, combine all of the ingredients except for the rolls and eggs. Set aside. Separate the rolls into 8 triangles. On a greased **COOKIE SHEET**, arrange the triangles in a circle, leaving a 2-inch hole in the middle of the ring, with the narrow tips pointing outward. Press the sides of the triangles together so that there are no gaps in the ring. Spoon the chicken salad mixture onto the center of the widest part of each triangle, making sure to pack it down firmly. Fold the dough tips inwards around the filling. Tuck under the ring. Brush the whole ring with the egg. Bake for 25 minutes.

Remove from the oven and allow to cool. Slice into individual pieces, and place on **DECORATIVE PLATES**. Serve warm.

Sweet & Sour Meatballs

FROM THE KITCHEN OF MARY GALES

1 POUND GROUND BEEF
1 EGG
1 TEASPOON SALT
1/2 TEASPOON BLACK PEPPER
3 TABLESPOONS GREEN ONIONS, DICED
3 TABLESPOONS CORNSTARCH
1 (8-OUNCE) CAN PINEAPPLE WEDGES
3 TABLESPOONS OIL
1 TABLESPOON SOY SAUCE
3 TABLESPOONS VINEGAR
1/3 CUP SUGAR
1/3 CUP WATER
2 GREEN PEPPERS, CUT INTO 1/2-INCH STRIPS

Mix together the beef, egg, salt, pepper, green onions, and 1 table-spoon of the cornstarch. Shape the mixture into marble-sized balls. Drain the pineapple, reserving the juice. Set aside.

Heat 2 tablespoons of the oil in a **SKILLET** and brown the meat-balls on all sides. Remove. Add the remaining oil to the skillet. Mix together the remaining cornstarch, the soy sauce, vinegar, sugar, water, and reserved pineapple juice. Add to the skillet and stir con-stantly until thickened. Add the pineapple wedges, green peppers, and meatballs. Bring to a boil and cook for 3 minutes more. Place the pineapple, green peppers, and meatballs on a **DECORATIVE SERVING PLATE**, and drizzle the sauce over the top. Serve with toothpicks.

Spicy Meatballs

FROM THE KITCHEN OF CATHY LEWIS

1 CUP OLD-FASHIONED OATS
3/4 CUP FAT FREE EVAPORATED MILK
1 MEDIUM ONION, CHOPPED
1 TEASPOON SALT
1 TEASPOON CHILI POWDER
1/4 TEASPOON GARLIC SALT
1/4 TEASPOON PEPPER
1 1/2 POUNDS LEAN TURKEY OR GROUND BEEF
NONSTICK COOKING SPRAY

SAUCE:
2 CUPS KETCHUP
1 1/2 CUPS BROWN SUGAR, PACKED
1/4 CUPS ONION, CHOPPED
2 TABLESPOONS LIQUID SMOKE
1/2 TEASPOON GARLIC SALT

Preheat the oven to 350° F. In a **MEDIUM BOWL**, combine the oats, milk, onion, salt, chili powder, garlic salt, and pepper. Crumble the meat into the mixture and mix well. Shape into 1-inch balls. Spray a **9X13-INCH BAKING DISH** with cooking spray and place the meatballs in the dish. Bake, uncovered, for 10-15 minutes.

To make the sauce, combine the sauce ingredients and mix well. Remove the meatballs from the oven, pour the sauce over the meatballs, and bake for 30-35 minutes more, or until the meatballs are cooked through. Serve warm on a **DECORATIVE SERVING PLATE**.

Homemade Sloppy Joes

FROM THE KITCHEN OF JUDY WESTRUM

2 POUNDS HAMBURGER
1 (6-OUNCE) CAN TOMATO PASTE
2 CUPS WATER
1 CUP KETCHUP
1 MEDIUM ONION, CHOPPED
2 TABLESPOONS BROWN SUGAR
1/2 TEASPOON MUSTARD
1/2 TEASPOON WORCESTERSHIRE SAUCE
6-8 HAMBURGER BUNS

In a **LARGE FRYING PAN**, brown the hamburger, about 5-7 minutes. Drain the excess liquid. Add the remaining ingredients, except for the hamburger buns, and simmer, uncovered, for 1 hour. Place the hamburger buns face open on **INDIVIDUAL SERVING PLATES**, generously spoon the hamburger mixture over the buns, and serve warm.

Vegetarian "Meat" Sandwiches

EMILY PRIDDY, President
Friends of the Mother Road

1 SMALL YELLOW ONION, DICED
2 TABLESPOONS OLIVE OIL
1 PACKAGE GIMME LEAN OR SIMILAR MEAT SUBSTITUTE
1 CUP LIGHT VEGETABLE BROTH
6-8 HAMBURGER BUNS

Over medium-high heat, sauté the onion in olive oil until the onion is clear. Add the Gimme Lean. Stir the Gimme Lean until it crumbles. Add in the broth and bring to a boil. Reduce the heat and let simmer, stirring occasionally, until all of the liquid evaporates.

Fill each hamburger bun with the Gimme Lean mixture and place on individual serving plates. Serve warm with mustard and pickles.

Friends in High Places

Heights don't scare me. They paralyze me. Always have. Halfway up a stepladder, I can't breathe. I can't think. My hips lock up, my legs won't move, and I start to shake. Sometimes I cry.

I've been that way since I was little. I hated riding the escalator at the mall, because I was afraid I might fall. I wouldn't climb the monkey bars at school, because I was afraid I might fall. It took me years to work up the nerve to ride the carousel at the carnival, much less the Ferris wheel. The only thing bigger than my fear of heights is my love of Route 66.

So it was that I came to be standing on a boom lift 30 feet above the ground last month, clinging to the railing for dear life with one hand while I scraped paint off an old motel sign with the other, confronting my fear in the name of historic preservation.

It was the most terrifying thing I have ever done, and when I was finally finished—the sign scraped and primed and a new coat of bright red and yellow paint blazing away in the early October sunshine—the first words out of my mouth were, "I hope I never have to do that again."

Three weeks later, I was standing on a platform at the top of a forklift 15 feet off the ground in a stiff Texas Panhandle wind, using the leftover paint to revitalize yet another historic sign.

My non-roadie friends think I'm nuts. They roll their eyes and laugh when I come into the office with aching muscles, peeling nose, and an envelope full of before-and-after photographs and tell them about the wonderful weekend I just spent standing in a chilly spring drizzle, squirting caulk into cracks on an old gas station, or standing in the hot August sun all day to sell handmade necklaces in the hopes of raising a few precious dollars for historic preservation. What's good about a sore back and a sunburn? Who'd want to spend a day working in the rain? And what kind of sucker wastes a weekend doing work, anyway?

There's no point in trying to explain it to them.

As far as I'm concerned, there are two kinds of people in this world: People who have a hammer in one hand and a tube of caulk in the other, and people who don't.

You don't have to explain it to the first group. They already get it.

You can't explain it to the second group. Words are a poor substitute for the comfort of a hot shower and a soft motel bed at the end of a long day of hard work…the paint smudge you wear on your face all weekend like a badge of honor…the satisfaction of driving past a Meramec Caverns barn and thinking, "I helped paint the S." Nothing tastes like a blue-plate special after a day on a ladder. Nothing feels like a celebratory hug at the end of a successful project. You can't explain it. You just have to get out there and try it.

But be forewarned: Once you've experienced the high of preservation, you can't quit. Thankfully, while this craving gets into your blood quickly and lingers there forever, the only long-term side effects are lasting friendships.

It may, however, be hazardous to your fears. Just last week, I caught myself wondering if it might not be possible to shimmy up the shafts of the Twin Arrows to replace their plywood "feathers." I've gotta get my fix of Route 66!

Diner Delights

This collection of amazing meals will warm your kitchen, comfort your family, and amaze your guests. Included are some of Route 66's favorite home-style, classic American recipes.

ROUTE 66 CHEESEBURGER

BLEU CHEESE BURGER

SURPRISE BURGERS

ROY'S DOUBLE CHEESEBURGER

BEER 'N' BRATS

CHILI ROJO

ROD'S RED CHILI CHOWDER

HENRY'S HOTTER THAN HELL CHILI

PEPPER STEAK

CHICKEN FRIED STEAK

VENISON STEAK MOLOKAI

CHALUPAS

SOUR CREAM ENCHILADAS

ITALIAN DELIGHT

MEAL-IN-ONE

OLD-FASHIONED MEATLOAF

SWEET & SAVORY BRISKET

COMPANY CHICKEN

THAI CHICKEN CURRY

ORANGE CASHEW CHICKEN

CHEESY CHICKEN BAKE

CHICKEN & DUMPLINGS

REVERSE POLLO RELLENO

CHICKEN FETTUCCINE ALFREDO

CHICKEN POT PIE

CHICKEN ENCHILADA CASSEROLE

TURKEY BROCCOLI HOLLANDAISE

BARBECUE TURKEY LOAF

FIRECRACKER SALMON STEAKS

SHRIMP CURRY

MANICOTTI

TORTELLINI CASSEROLE

VEGGIE STIR FRY

CAULIFLOWER BROCCOLI DISH

TORTILLA CASSEROLE

RATATOUILLE

ALTERNATIVE VEGETABLE BAKE

VEGETABLE CASSEROLE

Route 66 Cheeseburger with Honey Mustard BBQ Sauce

Jim Rowenhorst, Metro Diner
3001 E. 11th Street, Tulsa, OK 74101, (918) 592-2616

⅓ POUND GROUND BEEF, SHAPED INTO A 6 X 2-INCH PATTY
2 SLICES AMERICAN CHEESE
1 6-INCH HOAGIE BUN
2 LEAVES LETTUCE
½ MEDIUM TOMATO, SLICED
¼ ONION, SLICED

BBQ SAUCE:
1 QUART CATTLEMEN'S BBQ SAUCE
2 TABLESPOONS HONEY
1 CUP DIJON MUSTARD

Cook the burger to medium-well doneness. About 1 minute before removing from the heat, top with the cheese.

To make the sauce, mix all of the sauce ingredients together. Spread generously on each side of the bun. Place the lettuce, tomato slices, and onion on one side of the bun, and top with the hamburger. Place the top on the burger, and serve warm with French fries.

Bleu Cheese Burger

Jim Rowenhorst, Metro Diner
3001 E. 11th Street, Tulsa, OK 74101, (918) 592-2616

2 TABLESPOONS BLEU CHEESE, CRUMBLED
1/2 POUND LEAN GROUND BEEF
2 HAMBURGER BUNS
BLEU CHEESE DRESSING
4 LEAVES LETTUCE
1 MEDIUM TOMATO, SLICED

In a **SMALL BOWL**, mix the cheese and ground beef. Form two round patties out of the mixture. Cook or grill to desired doneness.

Meanwhile, toast the buns until lightly browned. Generously spread the bleu cheese dressing on each side of the bun. Dress the buns with lettuce and tomato slices. Place the cheeseburger on the buns and serve immediately.

Surprise Burgers

From the kitchen of Betty Marcus

1 POUND LEAN GROUND BEEF
2/3 CUP BELL PEPPER, DICED
2/3 CUP ONION, DICED
1/3 CUP GREEN OLIVES STUFFED WITH PIMIENTO, SLICED IN THIRDS
2/3 CUP FRESH TOMATO, DICED
1 CUP CHEDDAR CHEESE, SHREDDED
SALT, TO TASTE
BLACK PEPPER, TO TASTE
3-4 HAMBURGER BUNS

Place all ingredients in a **LARGE BOWL**, except for the hamburger buns, and mix together with your hands. Form into large patties. Broil to desired doneness on the oven broiler. (These patties must be broiled—do not put them on the grill.) Carefully turn the patties over once during broiling. Remove from the oven and place the patties on the hamburger buns. Serve immediately and enjoy!

Roy's Route 66 Double Cheeseburger

ROY'S MOTEL AND CAFÉ

Amboy, CA, www.rt66roys.com

The town of Amboy, which we own, is about 200 yards long on both sides of Route 66 in the middle of the Mojave Desert between Needles and Barstow. We have a PO Box, but there is no real address. To send us mail, you would label it: Roy's Motel and Café, PO Box 66H, Amboy, CA, 92304. Our phone number in Amboy is (760) 733-4263. Thanks, Roy.

It gets real darn hot here in Amboy. So hot, in fact, that we often cook our burgers on the hood of Sheriff Wilson's '63 Mercury. Contrary to popular belief, the secret ingredient in a Roy's Route 66 Double Cheeseburger is not desert roadkill. To prove it, I'm giving you the recipe that keeps the customers coming back for our legendary burgers.

8 OUNCES LEAN GROUND BEEF
4 SLICES GOOD OLD PROCESSED AMERICAN CHEESE
1 SESAME SEED BUN, LIGHTLY TOASTED
RELISH, TO TASTE
KETCHUP, TO TASTE
MUSTARD, TO TASTE
MAYONNAISE, TO TASTE
2 THIN SLICES RED ONION
4 THIN SLICES TOMATO
2 LEAVES CRISP LETTUCE, TORN

Divide the ground beef into 2 halves. Shape each half into a patty and grill to desired doneness. About 1 minute before removing the patties from the heat, add one slice of cheese on top of each patty.

Dress up the toasted bun with your favorite condiments, and then, doing one patty at a time, layer one slice of cheese, one onion slice, two slices of tomato, and one leaf of lettuce. Now repeat with the second patty. First add the cheese, and then one onion slice, two slices of tomato, and one leaf of lettuce. Now, stack the two layered patties on top of the bun and add the top. Hopefully, this is not too complicated for you. If it is, just stop by Roy's, and we'll make one up for you. Enjoy!

Beer 'n' Brats

FROM THE KITCHEN OF CATHY LEWIS

1/2 MEDIUM ONION, CHOPPED
1 GARLIC CLOVE, CHOPPED
1 TABLESPOON OLIVE OIL OR VEGETABLE
OIL (ADD MORE IF NEEDED)
SALT, TO TASTE
BLACK PEPPER, TO TASTE
2 BOTTLES BEER (THE BRAND AND TYPE
OF YOUR CHOICE)
4-6 BRATWURST

In a **LARGE FRYING PAN**, sauté the onions and garlic in the oil until light brown. Add the beer, salt, and pepper. Bring to a low boil. Add the bratwurst. Boil for 15-20 minutes. Remove the brats and grill for approximately 20 minutes, or until cooked through, turning about every 5 minutes. Serve hot with your favorite accompaniments.

Chili Rojo

LA CITA RESTAURANT
812 S. 1st Street, Tucumcari, NM 88401, (505) 461-0949

4 POUNDS GROUND BEEF
6 CLOVES GARLIC, CHOPPED
SALT, TO TASTE
BLACK PEPPER, TO TASTE
3/4 CUP ALL-PURPOSE FLOUR
1/4 CUP RED CHILI POWDER
2 TABLESPOONS CRUSHED RED PEPPER

In a **LARGE FRYING PAN**, brown the beef with the garlic, salt, and pepper, about 10-15 minutes. Drain the excess fat and add the flour. Return the pan to the heat and mix well. Add the red chili powder and the crushed red pepper. Stir in enough water to reach the desired consistency. Simmer for 45 minutes, or until the meat mixture is heated through. Serve hot with tortillas chips and fresh salsa.

Red Chili Chowder

LAWRENCE S. SANCHEZ & STELLA K. SANCHEZ, Rod's Steak House
301 East Route 66, Williams, AZ 86046, (928) 635-2671

1 POUND PINTO BEANS
4 STRIPS BACON, CHOPPED
SALT, TO TASTE
BLACK PEPPER, TO TASTE
1/4 TEASPOON GARLIC SALT
1/4 TEASPOON WHITE PEPPER
SEASONING SALT, TO TASTE
1/2 TEASPOON OREGANO
2 CUBES BEEF BOUILLON, OR 2 TEASPOONS
**   BEEF GRANULES**
1 TABLESPOON OIL
1 POUND GROUND BEEF
1 LARGE ONION, CHOPPED
2 CUPS ZUCCHINI, CHOPPED
6 CUPS POTATOES, CUBED
8-10 TEASPOONS ALL-PURPOSE FLOUR, DEPENDING
**   ON HOW THICK YOU WANT THE SOUP**
1 CARTON RED CHILI PURÉE (I USE BACA'S OR
**   BUENOS RED CHILI BRANDS)**
1 BAG FROZEN WHOLE KERNEL CORN

Add the beans, bacon, salt, black pepper, garlic salt, white pepper, seasoning salt, oregano, and beef bouillon to a **MEDIUM SOUP POT**. Cook over medium-high heat until the beans are tender.

Meanwhile, in a **LARGE FRYING PAN**, heat the oil until hot. Sauté the ground beef, onion, zucchini, and potatoes in the oil until tender and lightly brown. Add the flour, one teaspoon at a time, to the meat mixture to soak up the oil and thicken the soup. Add the cooked beans and the stock to the meat mixture in the frying pan. Mix well. Add the red chili purée and the corn and mix well. Simmer all of the ingredients together for approximately 20 minutes, or until heated through. Enjoy!

Welcome!

Rod, or Rodney Graves, was born in Spruce Head, Maine in 1904. When Rod was eleven, he moved to California with his family. Later, he attended Stanford University. During the hardships of the twenties, he was forced to leave college. Since he was a lover of the great outdoors, it was natural for him to become a surveyor for the U. S. Coastal and Geodetic Survey. His and his crew's names are inscribed on the altitude marker on top of Mt. Lassen, and from there they thoroughly surveyed the California-Arizona-Mexico borders. After deciding to stay in Arizona, Rod bought and operated a small café in Seligman, a small community 48 miles west of Williams. This is where he met his future bride, Helen. After a short time, he sold this operation and set off for Phoenix with Helen, where she was a teacher. Helen and Rod were married in 1938. The both loved Northern Arizona, especially Williams and Prescott. After much deliberation, they decided Williams would be the site of their new home. Rod bought the Grand Canyon Tavern, which he operated for nearly seven years. During this business venture, Rod had the opportunity to meet many new townspeople and tourists. It was then Rod determined that a restaurant, perhaps a steak house, was needed in town. He sold the tavern and obtained the property to build and fulfill his dream.

On August 23, 1946, Rod, along with Helen, opened Rod's Steak House, which is located on Historic Route 66. The registered trademark menu, die cut in the shape of a steer, is the same one Rod used to open the Steak House back then (with, of course, a few minor changes). Rod operated his Steak House for the next 21 years. In August of 1967, Rod bowed out of the restaurant business.

Rod's Steak House has had three owners since that time. The third and current owners are Lawrence and Stella Sanchez. Mr. Sanchez, born almost exactly one year prior to the original opening of the restaurant, is a lifelong resident of Williams. During his teen years, Mr. Sanchez was employed by Rod Graves as a dishwasher and busboy! In 1969, Lawrence and Stella were married, and in January 1973, Lawrence went back to work at Rod's Steak House, this time as a manager. Mr. Sanchez worked as manager and head chef for the next 13 years. In August 1985, Lawrence and Stella bought Rod's Steak House. Having such a long term association with the restaurant and even with Rod Graves himself, Mr. Sanchez continues Rod's fine tradition. Today, Lawrence and Stella operate the restaurant and can be found here on almost every day and night of the year.

49

Henry's Hotter Than Hell Chili

Roy's Motel and Café
Amboy, CA, www.rt66roys.com

Before you try this chili take this test:
1. Are you brave?
2. Can you walk across hot coals in bare feet?
3. Is your stomach made of iron?
If you answered "NO" to any of these questions, proceed with extreme caution, arm yourself with plenty of ice water, and remember...we warned you!

2 CUPS OLIVE OIL
2 CUPS ONIONS, COARSELY CHOPPED
7 CLOVES GARLIC, MINCED
2 POUNDS GROUND BEEF CHUCK
2 GREEN PEPPERS, CORED, SEEDED, AND COARSELY CHOPPED
2 RED PEPPERS, CORED, SEEDED, AND COARSELY CHOPPED
5 JALAPEÑO CHILES, CORED, SEEDED, AND DICED
3 (3-OUNCE) CANS PLUM TOMATOES, DRAINED
1 CUP PARSLEY, CHOPPED
2 TABLESPOONS TOMATO PASTE
6 TABLESPOONS CHILI POWDER
3 TABLESPOONS GROUND CUMIN
2 TABLESPOONS DRIED OREGANO
1 TABLESPOON DRIED BASIL
2 TEASPOONS SALT
2 TEASPOONS FRESHLY GROUND BLACK PEPPER
2 POUNDS RIPE PLUM TOMATOES, QUARTERED
MONTEREY JACK CHEESE, SHREDDED
SOUR CREAM
GREEN ONIONS, SLICED

Heat the oil in a **DEEP, HEAVY, FLAMEPROOF CASSEROLE DISH** over low heat. Add the onions and garlic and cook for 5 minutes, or until clear. Raise the heat to medium, and add the ground beef. Stir frequently until the pieces are well broken up and the meat is brown. Add the bell peppers and jalapeños, stirring frequently until they are soft, approximately 10 minutes.

Remove the mixture from the heat, and stir in the drained tomatoes, parsley, tomato paste, and all the herbs and spices. Return the mixture to medium heat and cook, stirring frequently, for 10 minutes. Add the fresh tomatoes and cook for another 10 minutes.

Now it's ready to serve! Just add garnishes to your liking, and look out!

Pepper Steak

FROM THE KITCHEN OF MARY GALES

1 1/2 POUNDS BEEF SIRLOIN STEAK
1/2 CUP VEGETABLE OIL
1 CUP WATER
1 MEDIUM ONION, CUT INTO SLICES
1/2 TEASPOON GARLIC SALT
1/4 TEASPOON GINGER
2 MEDIUM GREEN PEPPERS, SEEDED AND CUT INTO STRIPS
1 BOX UNCOOKED INSTANT RICE
1 TABLESPOON CORNSTARCH
2 TEASPOONS SUGAR
2 TABLESPOONS SOY SAUCE
2 MEDIUM TOMATOES, EACH CUT INTO EIGHT PIECES

Trim the fat off the beef. Cut the beef into strips approximately 2x1-inches thick. Heat the oil in a **LARGE SKILLET**. Add the beef and cook, turning frequently, until brown, about 5 minutes. Stir in the water, onion, garlic salt, and ginger. Heat to boiling, and then reduce the heat. Cover and simmer for 5-8 minutes. Add the green pepper strips during last 5 minutes of simmering.

Meanwhile, cook the instant rice as directed on the box. Set aside. In a **SMALL BOWL**, blend the cornstarch, sugar, and soy sauce. Stir into the beef mixture. Cook, stirring constantly, until the mixture thickens and boils. Boil and stir for 1 minute. Add the tomato pieces and continue to cook until the tomatoes are heated through, about 3 minutes. Spoon the rice onto **INDIVIDUAL SERVING PLATES**. Cover with the steak mixture and serve hot.

Chicken Fried Steak: Dedra's Beer Batter Recipe

CHARLIE'S CORNER CAFÉ
401 N. Main Street, Luther, OK (405) 277-9205

4 CUPS ALL-PURPOSE FLOUR
4 EGGS
1 (12-OUNCE) CAN BEER (I PREFER MILWAUKEE'S BEST ICE)
2 TEASPOONS BARON GARLIC PEPPER
1/2 TEASPOON CELERY SALT
1 TEASPOON LAWREY'S SEASON-ALL
1 TEASPOON SALT
MILK, ENOUGH TO THIN TO A PANCAKE MIX CONSISTENCY
18-20 (4-OUNCE) CUBE STEAKS

In a **LARGE BOWL**, combine all of the ingredients together except for the steaks. Mix very well. Doing one steak at a time, dip each steak in the batter, making sure that the batter sticks. In a **LARGE DEEP-FRYER**, deep fry the steaks until cooked through. Serve immediately with your favorite side dish.

Many people think Luther is a nowhere town with nothing of interest. The truth is that we have hidden treasures like Charlie's Corner Café, where you'll find great home cooking. From our tender flaky chicken frys to our gigantic old-fashioned hamburgers made from fresh ground beef, you can't beat our low prices and friendly faces.

This café was brought back to life by partners and friends, Charley Briscoe and Dedra Turnbough. Even though our dear friend Charley passed away not long after the place was running, Dedra still makes it work in his name. All of the décor in Charley's Café was given to the café by local townspeople. So come on in and see our cozy little Corner Café in Luther, Oklahoma on Main Street. Whether you just want a hot cup of Jo or a big breakfast or lunch, you'll find what your want here.

Venison Steak Molokai

FROM THE KITCHEN OF NESSA SHUE

8 (8-OUNCE) VENISON OR BEEF STEAKS

MARINADE:
1 CUP OLIVE OIL
2 CUPS RED WINE
1 CUP ONION, CHOPPED
1 CUP CARROTS, SLICED
1 CUP CELERY, CHOPPED
4 CLOVES GARLIC, CRUSHED
1 TABLESPOONS PEPPERCORNS
6 BAY LEAVES
8 CLOVES
1/2 TEASPOON ROSEMARY
1/4 TEASPOON THYME
1/4 TEASPOON OREGANO

SAUCE:
1/3 CUP CLARIFIED BUTTER
1 TEASPOON SALT
4 TABLESPOONS BRANDY
1 TABLESPOON ALL-PURPOSE FLOUR
1 TEASPOON BEEF BASE
1/2 CUP WHIPPING CREAM
1/2 CUP SOUR CREAM

In a **LARGE BOWL**, combine all of the marinade ingredients. Marinate the steaks for 48 hours in the refrigerator, turning occasionally.

Remove the steaks from the marinade and pat dry. Reserve the marinade. In a **LARGE FRYING PAN**, sauté 4 steaks at a time in the butter. Season with salt. After all of the steaks have been sautéed, return them all to the pan, add the brandy, and flame. When the flame dies, place the steaks on a warm platter.

Meanwhile, stir the flour into the pan drippings. Add the reserved marinade and beef base and simmer until the liquid is reduced by 1/3. Add the whipping cream and sour cream. Simmer for 1-2 minutes and taste for seasoning. Pour the sauce over the steaks and serve warm.

DINER DELIGHTS

Chalupas

LA CITA RESTAURANT
812 S. 1st Street, Tucumcari, NM 88401, (505) 461-0949

1 POUND GROUND BEEF
6 CLOVES GARLIC
1 TEASPOON ONION POWDER
1/2 TEASPOON SEASONING SALT
VEGETABLE OIL
12 (6-INCH) CORN TORTILLAS
1 CUP COOKED PINTO BEANS
2 CUPS LETTUCE, SHREDDED
2 MEDIUM TOMATOES, CHOPPED
1 CUP MOZZARELLA CHEESE, SHREDDED
1/4 CUP BLACK OLIVES, SLICED
SOUR CREAM
GUACAMOLE

In a **MEDIUM SKILLET**, brown the ground beef with garlic, onion powder, and seasoning salt. Set aside. In the same skillet, add 1/2-inch of oil, and fry the tortillas until crisp. Layer each fried tortilla with the ground beef mixture, pinto beans, lettuce, tomato, and cheese. Top with black olives, sour cream, and guacamole. Serve immediately!

Sour Cream Enchiladas

FROM THE KITCHEN OF ROBIN WRIGHT

2   (14-OUNCE) CANS CREAM OF CHICKEN SOUP
2   (4-OUNCE) CANS GREEN CHILES
1   CUP SOUR CREAM
12 (6-INCH) CORN TORTILLAS
1   POUND HAMBURGER, BROWNED
**   CHEDDAR CHEESE, SHREDDED**

Preheat the oven to 350° F. In a **LARGE PAN**, mix the soup, chiles, and sour cream. Cook over low heat until heated through. Set aside. In a **SEPARATE FRYING PAN**, add 1/2-inch of oil, and fry the tortillas until lightly brown, but still flexible. Fill each tortilla with 1–2 tablespoons of the hamburger and cheese. Roll and place in **9X13-INCH CASSEROLE DISH**. Pour the soup mixture over the enchiladas and top with more cheese. Bake for 20 minutes, or until thoroughly heated. Scoop out 2 enchiladas onto each plate and serve warm with a side of tortilla chips.

Italian Delight

FROM THE KITCHEN OF DIANA LEPPKE

6 OUNCES DRY WIDE NOODLES
1 POUND GROUND BEEF
1 LARGE ONION, CHOPPED
1/2 GREEN BELL PEPPER, CHOPPED
1 (8-OUNCE) CAN TOMATO SAUCE
1/8 TEASPOON TABASCO
1 (16-OUNCE) CAN CREAM CORN
1 SMALL CAN SLICED BLACK OLIVES
2 TEASPOONS WORCESTERSHIRE SAUCE
1 CUP CANNED TOMATOES
1 1/2 TEASPOON SALT
1 TEASPOON GARLIC SALT
2 CUPS CHEDDAR CHEESE, GRATED

Preheat the oven to 350° F. Cook the noodles in boiling salted water for 8 minutes. Rinse and drain them, and set aside. Lightly brown the meat in a **MEDIUM SKILLET**. Add the onion and green pepper and cook until the vegetables are tender.

In a **LARGE BOWL**, combine the noodles, meat mixture, and all the remaining ingredients, except 1 cup of the cheese, mixing well. Turn into a greased **2 1/2-QUART CASSEROLE DISH**. Bake for 45 minutes. Sprinkle the remaining cheese over the top and bake for about 10 minutes longer. Serve immediately.

A Meal-in-One

FROM THE KITCHEN OF BETTY MARCUS

1 POUND LEAN GROUND BEEF
1 MEDIUM ONION, CHOPPED
1 TABLESPOON OIL
1 LARGE CAN WHOLE TOMATOES, WITH THE JUICE
1 CAN CORN, WITH THE JUICE
1 CAN CHOPPED BLACK OLIVES, WITH THE JUICE
2 CUPS ZITI
NONSTICK COOKING SPRAY
CHEDDAR CHEESE, GRATED
SALT, TO TASTE
BLACK PEPPER, TO TASTE

Preheat the oven to 350° F. In a **LARGE POT**, cook the ground beef and onion in the cooking oil until the meat is no longer pink and the onions are beginning to soften. Add the tomatoes with the juice, the corn with juice, and the olives with juice. Stir in the uncooked noodles, mix well, and simmer, about 8 minutes.

Spray a **9X13-INCH BAKING DISH** with cooking spray. Pour the meat mixture into the dish and bake for about 45 minutes, or until bubbly. About 10 minutes before you remove the casserole, add the grated cheese. Allow to cool for 5 minutes, and then serve warm.

Note: This recipe should be made, simmered on the stovetop, and then immediately cooked in the oven. If you do the assembly process earlier in the day, the noodles get very mushy. This recipe is so easy to make that doing it about one hour before you plan to eat shouldn't be a problem.

Old-fashioned Meatloaf

PEGGY SUE'S DINER
We are located 8 miles north of Barstow on the I-15 Highway,
Ghost Town Road, Calico Ghost Town

2 POUNDS GROUND BEEF
1/2 ONION, MINCED
1 1/2 STALKS CELERY, MINCED
1 1/2 TEASPOONS GARLIC POWDER
1 1/2 TEASPOONS LAWREY'S SEASONING SALT
1 1/2 TEASPOONS BLACK PEPPER
2 EGGS, BEATEN
1 CUP SALTINE CRACKERS, CRUSHED
2 TABLESPOONS WORCESTERSHIRE SAUCE
2 TABLESPOONS SOY SAUCE

Preheat the oven to 350° F. In a **LARGE BOWL**, mix all of the ingredients together with a wooden spoon. Form into a loaf. Place the meatloaf in a **ROASTING PAN** (do not use a loaf pan, as the outside edges are crispier in a roasting pan). Brush the outside of the loaf with your favorite kitchen bouquet sauce or Worcestershire sauce. Bake for 1 hour. Remove from the oven, slice, and serve warm.

This meal is perfect for serving for multiple days. Our suggestion is to serve meatloaf dinner the first day, a hot meatloaf sandwich the second day, and cold meatloaf with ketchup on white bread the third day. It's delicious no matter how you serve it!

Here at Peggy Sue's Diner we serve old-fashioned comfort food made from my grandmother Ollie Buries' recipes. She fixed three meals a day for eighty years. She went to Heaven last year at the age of ninety-seven after a full, healthy life that was rich with family, good food, and love. She always made good food from inexpensive ingredients and meats, always boiling a pot of beans with a ham hock or salt pork. I still cook like that, as I did while raising my family of six. I hate to see a family paying the same price for fast food that I spend to make a hearty, homemade meal. Of course, now I appreciate cooking as an art and a very gratifying hobby. It is the art of creation and offers instant pleasure!

Sweet & Savory Brisket

FROM THE KITCHEN OF MARILYN SEUMPTEWA

1 (3-POUND) BEEF BRISKET, CUT IN HALF
1 CUP KETCHUP
1/4 CUP GRAPE JELLY
1 PACKAGE ONION SOUP MIX
1/2 TEASPOON BLACK PEPPER

Place half of the brisket in a **SLOW COOKER.** In a bowl, combine the ketchup, jelly, soup mix, and pepper. Pour it over the meat in the slow cooker. Cover and cook on low for 8-10 hours, or until the meat is tender. Serve with your favorite vegetables on the side.

Company Chicken

FROM THE KITCHEN OF ROBIN WRIGHT

1 (5-OUNCE) PACKAGE CHIPPED BEEF, CUT UP
8-10 BONELESS, SKINLESS CHICKEN BREASTS
8-10 SLICES BACON
1/2 PINT SOUR CREAM
2 (14-OUNCE) CANS CREAM OF MUSHROOM SOUP
1 CUP MILK

Preheat the oven to 350° F. Butter a **9X13-INCH CASSEROLE DISH**. Put the chipped beef on the bottom of the dish. Wrap each chicken breast with slice of bacon and place on top of the chipped beef.

In a **MEDIUM BOWL**, mix together the sour cream, the soup, and the milk. Pour over the top of the chicken and bake for 1 hour. Serve over long grain rice.

Thai Chicken Curry

FROM THE KITCHEN OF NESSA SHUE

**3 POUNDS SKINLESS, BONELESS CHICKEN
BREASTS, CUBED
2 TABLESPOONS CORNSTARCH
1 MEDIUM ONION, DICED
1 CLOVE GARLIC, MINCED
1/4 CUP BUTTER
1 TEASPOON CURRY POWDER
1 TABLESPOON FRESH GINGER, MINCED
1 (12-OUNCE) CAN FROZEN COCONUT
MILK, THAWED
1 TABLESPOON THAI FISH SAUCE
2 SMALL ZUCCHINIS, DICED
1/2 CUP FRESH MINT LEAVES
4 GREEN ONIONS, THINLY SLICED
1 TEASPOON CRUSHED RED PEPPER
SALT, TO TASTE
BLACK PEPPER, TO TASTE**

Coat the chicken with cornstarch. Set aside. In a **LARGE SKILLET** or **WOK**, sauté the onions and garlic in butter until soft. Add the chicken, curry powder, and ginger and stir-fry for 2 minutes. Add the coconut milk, fish sauce, and zucchini and simmer for 3 minutes more. Add the remaining ingredients and simmer for 1 minute. Serve warm over rice.

Orange Cashew Chicken

FROM THE KITCHEN OF MARILYN SEUMPTEWA

**1 POUND BONELESS, SKINLESS CHICKEN BREASTS,
CUT INTO 1-INCH CUBES
2 MEDIUM CARROTS, SLICED
1/2 CUP CELERY, CHOPPED
2 TABLESPOONS VEGETABLE OIL
2 TABLESPOONS CORNSTARCH
1/4 TEASPOON GROUND GINGER
3/4 CUP ORANGE JUICE
1/4 CUP HONEY
3 TEASPOON SOY SAUCE
1/2 CUP SALTED CASHEWS**

In a **LARGE SKILLET** or **WOK**, stir-fry the chicken, carrots, and celery in the oil for 8-10 minutes, or until the juices run clear. Reduce the heat. In a **SMALL BOWL**, combine the cornstarch, ginger, orange juice, honey, and soy sauce. Mix until well blended. Stir into the chicken mixture. Bring to a boil. Cook and stir for 2 minutes more, or until thickened. Stir in the cashews. Serve over rice.

Cheesy Chicken Bake

FROM THE KITCHEN OF MARY LAYCHAK

**3-4 SKINLESS, BONELESS CHICKEN BREASTS
1/2 CUP OLIVE OIL
1/2 CUP PARMESAN CHEESE
1 CUP ITALIAN BREAD CRUMBS
1 TEASPOON GARLIC POWDER**

Preheat the oven to 350° F. Pour the oil into a **MEDIUM BOWL** and set aside. In a **SEPARATE BOWL**, combine the cheese, bread crumbs, and garlic powder. Dip each chicken breast in the oil, making sure it is completely coated, and then dip the chicken in the bread crumb mixture. Place each coated chicken breast in a **BAKING PAN**. Bake for 30 minutes, or until the chicken is cooked through. Serve with a side of rice and fresh bread.

Don't Forget Winona Chicken and Dumplings

FROM THE KITCHEN OF ERIC HOWARD

1 WHOLE CHICKEN
4 CUPS WATER
2 CUPS CHICKEN BROTH
1 BAY LEAF
2 CARROTS, COARSELY CHOPPED
2 STALKS CELERY, COARSELY CHOPPED
1 ONION, QUARTERED
1/2 TEASPOON SALT
1/4 TEASPOON FRESHLY GROUND BLACK PEPPER
1 CUP MILK

DUMPLINGS:
2 CUPS FLOUR
1/2 TEASPOON BAKING SODA
1/2 TEASPOON SALT
3 TABLESPOONS VEGETABLE SHORTENING
3/4 CUPS BUTTERMILK

Place the chicken in a **LARGE POT**. Add the water, chicken broth, bay leaf, carrots, celery, onion, and salt. Bring to a boil, cover, and lower the heat. Simmer for about 1 hour, or until the chicken is tender and cooked through.

Saving the liquid, remove the chicken and allow to cool slightly. Remove and reserve the carrots. Remove the onion, celery, and bay leaf and discard. Allow the remaining liquid to settle, and then strain away any remaining solids. Set aside the strained liquid.

When the chicken is cool, remove the meat from the bone by tearing or cutting it into bite-sized chunks. Discard the bones. Mix the reserved carrots with the chicken and set aside.

In a **SMALL BOWL**, combine the flour, baking soda, and the salt. Cut in the shortening with wooden spoons or two knives. Add the buttermilk, and stir until the dry ingredients are moist. Turn the dough out on a floured surface and knead 5-6 times, NO MORE! Pat the dough down to 1/2-inch thickness. Set aside.

Bring the reserved chicken broth to a low boil, stir in the pepper and milk. Season to taste. Pinch or cut off 1 1/2-inch pieces of dough and gently drop them into the boiling broth. Stir gently with a wooden spoon, making sure the dumplings don't stick together. Cook the dumplings for 8-10 minutes, or until tender. Add the reserved chicken and carrot mixture and simmer until heated. Serve immediately.

61

Reverse Pollo Relleno

FROM THE KITCHENS OF STACEY EDGAR AND SADIE THOMAS

1 ¹/₂ POUNDS SKINLESS, BONELESS
   CHICKEN BREASTS
¹/₃ CUP CORNMEAL
2 TABLESPOONS TACO SEASONING
1 EGG WHITE
1 (4-OUNCE) CAN WHOLE GREEN CHILES,
   RINSED, SEEDED, AND CUT IN HALF
2 OUNCES MONTEREY JACK CHEESE, CUT
   INTO 2 ¹/₂-INCH SLICES
¹/₄ TEASPOON CRUSHED RED PEPPER

Preheat the oven to 375° F. Rinse the chicken and pat dry. Place each breast between 2 pieces of plastic wrap. Pound lightly until they are 1/8-inch thick. Set aside.

In a **SMALL BOWL,** combine the cornmeal and taco seasoning. In **ANOTHER BOWL**, separate the egg, and lightly beat the egg white.

Lay the chicken flat, and place half a chile on each piece of chicken. Place the cheese slices on the chile near the edge. Sprinkle with crushed red pepper. Fold the sides in and start rolling. Brush the chicken rolls with the egg, and then coat with the cornmeal mixture. Place the rolls, seam side down, in a shallow **BAKING PAN**. Bake, uncovered, for 25-30 minutes, or until the chicken is cooked through. If desired, serve with salsa or shredded cheese on top.

Chicken Fettuccine Alfredo

FROM THE KITCHEN OF CATHY LEWIS

8 OUNCES FETTUCCINE PASTA
5 CUPS BROCCOLI FLORETS
1 TABLESPOON BUTTER OR MARGARINE
1 1/2 CUPS RED BELL PEPPER, CUT INTO 3/4-INCH PIECES
2 CLOVES GARLIC, MINCED
1/2 MEDIUM ONION, CHOPPED
1 (1 1/2-OUNCE) PACKAGE ALFREDO SAUCE MIX
1 3/4 CUPS REDUCED FAT MILK
1/4 CUP WHITE WINE
1/2 TEASPOON MUSTARD POWDER
3-4 SKINLESS, BONELESS CHICKEN BREASTS,
    FULLY COOKED
1/3 CUP PARMESAN CHEESE, GRATED

Cook the pasta according to package directions, adding the broccoli during the last 2 minutes of cooking time. Drain and set aside.

Meanwhile, in a **LARGE SKILLET**, melt the butter over medium heat. Add the bell peppers, garlic, and onion. Cook until softened, about 10 minutes. Stir in the dry sauce mix, milk, wine, and mustard. Bring to a boil. Cook until thickened, about 5 minutes. Add the chicken and Parmesan and cook until heated through, about 2-3 minutes. Add the pasta and broccoli to the skillet and mix well. Transfer to a **LARGE SERVING DISH** and serve warm.

Chicken Pot Pie

FROM THE KITCHEN OF ALMA SCHNAPP

POT PIE:
2 TABLESPOONS SHORTENING
2 CUPS FLOUR
1 TEASPOON SALT
1 EGG, BEATEN
³/4 CUP MILK

BROTH:
1 WHOLE CHICKEN
1 SMALL ONION, CHOPPED
2 STALKS CELERY, CHOPPED
1 MEDIUM POTATO, CUBED

To make the pot pie squares, cut the shortening into the flour with a fork to make "little ball" like consistency. Add the salt, egg, and milk. Roll out the dough until it is nice and thin. Cut into small squares. Put little holes in center of each square so they don't curl up. Set aside.

In a **LARGE SOUP POT**, place the whole chicken, onions, and celery. Add enough water to cover. Bring to a boil and cook until the chicken is cooked through. Remove the chicken, onion, and celery, take the chicken off the bone, and place back in the broth. Bring to a boil. Carefully drop in the pot pie squares, and simmer, covered, for about 20 minutes. Add the chopped potato, return to a boil, and cook until tender. Serve immediately.

Chicken Enchilada Casserole

FROM THE KITCHEN OF ROBIN WRIGHT

1 (14-OUNCE) CAN CREAM OF CHICKEN SOUP
³/4 CUP MILK
¹/2 CUP ONION, CHOPPED
1 SMALL CAN DICED GREEN CHILES
6 (6-INCH) CORN TORTILLAS
2 CUPS COOKED CHICKEN, CUBED
1 CUP CHEDDAR CHEESE, SHREDDED

Preheat the oven to 350° F. In a **MEDIUM MIXING BOWL**, combine the soup, milk, onion, and green chiles. Cut the tortillas into thick, 1 1/2-inch strips. In an **8X8-INCH BAKING DISH**, layer the tortillas, chicken, soup mixture, and cheese. Repeat the layers. Bake, covered, for 1 hour. Allow to cool slightly, and then serve warm with tortilla chips and fresh salsa on the side.

Turkey Broccoli Hollandaise

FROM THE KITCHEN OF MARILYN SEUMPTEWA

1 CUP FRESH BROCCOLI FLORETS
1 (6-OUNCE) PACKAGE STUFFING MIX
1 ENVELOPE HOLLANDAISE SAUCE
2 CUPS COOKED TURKEY OR CHICKEN, CUBED
1 (3-OUNCE) CAN FRENCH-FRIED ONIONS

Preheat the oven to 325° F. Place 1 inch of water and the broccoli in a **SAUCEPAN**. Bring to a boil. Reduce the heat, cover, and simmer for 5-8 minutes, or until crisp-tender.

Meanwhile, prepare the stuffing and sauce mixes according to package directions. Spoon the stuffing into a greased **11X7X2-INCH BAKING DISH**. Top with the cooked turkey. Drain the broccoli and arrange over the turkey. Spoon the hollandaise sauce over the top, and sprinkle with onions. Bake, uncovered, for 25-30 minutes, or until heated through. Serve warm.

Barbecue Turkey Loaf

FROM THE KITCHEN OF ROBIN WRIGHT

1 1/2 POUNDS LEAN GROUND TURKEY
1 (8-OUNCE) CAN SALT-FREE TOMATO SAUCE
1 CUP ONION, FINELY CHOPPED
SALT, TO TASTE
1/4 TEASPOON BLACK PEPPER
1/4 TEASPOON GARLIC POWDER
2 TEASPOONS WORCESTERSHIRE SAUCE
2 TABLESPOONS FIRMLY PACKED BROWN SUGAR
2 TABLESPOONS PREPARED YELLOW MUSTARD
1 TABLESPOON VINEGAR

Preheat the oven to 350° F. In a **LARGE BOWL**, combine the turkey, half of the tomato sauce, onion, salt, pepper, garlic powder, and Worcestershire sauce. Mix well. Put into a **LOAF PAN** and bake, uncovered, for 20 minutes. In **ANOTHER BOWL**, combine the remaining tomato sauce, brown sugar, mustard, and vinegar. Pour over loaf. Return the loaf to the oven and bake, uncovered, for 40 minutes longer. Remove from the oven, allow to cool slightly, slice, and serve warm.

Firecracker Salmon Steaks

FROM THE KITCHEN OF CATHY LEWIS

¹/₄ CUP BALSAMIC VINEGAR
¹/₄ CUP CHILI SAUCE
¹/₄ CUP PACKED BROWN SUGAR
3 GARLIC CLOVES, MINCED
2 TEASPOONS FRESH PARSLEY, MINCED
¹/₄ TEASPOON GROUND GINGER, OR 1 TEASPOON FRESH
   GINGERROOT, MINCED
¹/₄ TEASPOON CAYENNE PEPPER
¹/₄ TEASPOON CRUSHED RED PEPPER FLAKES, OPTIONAL
4 (6-OUNCE) SALMON STEAKS

In a **SMALL BOWL**, combine all of the ingredients except for the salmon. Coat the grill rack with nonstick cooking spray before starting the grill. Coat each piece of salmon with the sauce. Grill the salmon, uncovered, over medium heat for 4-5 minutes on each side, or until the fish flakes easily with a fork, brushing occasionally with sauce. Serve immediately with a little of the remaining sauce drizzled over the top.

Shrimp Curry

FROM THE KITCHEN OF CATHY LEWIS

4 OUNCES COCONUT
2 CUPS SKIM MILK
1 TEASPOON OLIVE OIL
1 CLOVE GARLIC, MINCED
1/4 CUP ONION, DICED
1/4 CUP CELERY, DICED
1/4 CUP APPLE, DICED
2 TABLESPOONS CURRY POWDER
2 TEASPOON SALT
4 WHOLE CLOVES
1 WHOLE STICK CINNAMON
1 1/2 POUNDS COOKED SHRIMP
1 1/2 TABLESPOONS CORNSTARCH
2 CUPS COOKED RICE

In a **SAUCE PAN**, bring the coconut and skim milk to a gentle boil over medium heat. Cover and let stand 30 minutes. Remove the lid and, reserving both, separate the coconut from liquid.

Heat the oil in a **SKILLET** over medium heat. Add the garlic, onion, celery, and apple. Sauté until tender. Add the reserved coconut and mix well. Stir in the curry powder, reserved coconut liquid, salt, cloves, and cinnamon. Cover and simmer on low for 15-20 minutes. Add the cooked shrimp and mix well.

In a **SEPARATE BOWL**, combine the cornstarch and a little cold water to make a smooth paste. Stir the cornstarch mixture into the other ingredients and blend well. Cover with the vapor valve closed and cook on low heat for an additional 15-20 minutes. Remove the cloves and cinnamon stick and discard.

Cook the rice according to package directions. Spoon out onto **INDIVIDUAL SERVING PLATES**. Spoon the curry over the hot rice. Garnish as desired with chopped peanuts, cashews, raisins, shredded coconut, chopped olives, or banana chips.

Manicotti

From the kitchen of Mary Gales

$1/2$ CUP ALL-PURPOSE FLOUR
2 EGGS PLUS 1 EGG, WELL BEATEN
1 TABLESPOON BUTTER, MELTED
$2/3$ CUP MILK
$1/2$ TEASPOON SALT
$1/2$ POUND RICOTTA CHEESE
$1/4$ CUP PARSLEY, CHOPPED
$1/4$ CUP PARMESAN CHEESE, GRATED
3 CUPS SPAGHETTI MEAT SAUCE

Preheat the oven to 375° F. In a **MEDIUM BOWL**, mix the flour, 2 of the eggs, melted butter, milk, and salt. Using a small ladle, spoon ladlefuls of batter into a small, hot greased **SKILLET**. Tilt the skillet around to make each pancake as thin as possible. Bake until done on one side only. Slide the pancake onto waxed paper and proceed with the next one.

To make the filling, mix the ricotta cheese, parsley, 1 egg, and Parmesan cheese. Spread a spoonful of mixture on each pancake, roll it up, and arrange in a baking dish. Pour 1 $1/2$ cups of the spaghetti meat sauce over the top. Bake for 20 minutes. Spoon out as many pieces as you desire, and serve with additional sauce on the top.

Tortellini Casserole

From the kitchen of Karen Billideau

1 STICK BUTTER
2 TABLESPOONS ALL-PURPOSE FLOUR
1 (10-OUNCE) CAN CHICKEN BROTH
1 PINT WHIPPING CREAM
1 CUP PARMESAN CHEESE, GRATED
SALT, TO TASTE
BLACK PEPPER, TO TASTE
DASH NUTMEG
2 PACKAGES TORTELLINI, COOKED

Preheat the oven to 350° F. In a **MEDIUM SKILLET**, melt the butter and add the flour. Add the chicken broth and stir until heated through. Add the whipping cream, cheese, salt, and pepper. Simmer for 3 minutes and then add the nutmeg. Put the cooked tortellini into a greased **9X13-INCH CASSEROLE DISH**. Pour the sauce over the top and bake for 40 minutes. This is an amazingly delicious dish!

Veggie Stir Fry

FROM THE KITCHEN OF CATHY LEWIS

4 TABLESPOONS CORNSTARCH
4 TABLESPOONS BROWN SUGAR
1/2 CUP SHERRY
5 TABLESPOONS SOY SAUCE
2 TABLESPOONS VEGETABLE OIL
1 CUP ONIONS, SLICED
1 YELLOW BELL PEPPER, SLICED
1 RED BELL PEPPER, SLICED
4 OUNCES SNOW PEAS
1 CUP BABY CORN
1 CUP MUSHROOMS, SLICED

In a **SMALL BOWL**, blend together the cornstarch, sugar, sherry, and soy sauce. Set aside. Heat the oil in a **WOK** or **SKILLET** and stir fry the vegetables over high heat for 2-3 minutes. Stir in the cornstarch mixture and cook until the sauce has slightly thickened. Serve over a bed of hot rice.

Cauliflower Broccoli Dish

FROM THE KITCHEN OF KATHY SWANSON

DRESSING:
1 CUP MAYONNAISE
1/2 CUP SUGAR
1/4 CUP PARMESAN CHEESE, GRATED

SALAD:
1 HEAD CAULIFLOWER, COARSELY CHOPPED
1 HEAD BROCCOLI, COARSELY CHOPPED
1 SMALL ONION, CHOPPED
1 POUND BACON, COOKED AND CRUMBLED

In a **SMALL BOWL**, mix together the dressing ingredients. Chill until ready to serve. In a **SEPARATE BOWL**, mix together the salad ingredients. Pour the dressing over the salad and mix until coated. Serve immediately.

Note: If you aren't planning on serving the whole salad at once, spoon out the desired amount into individual bowls, and pour the dressing over the top of each salad. Reserve the rest for later use. This will keep the salad from getting too soft.

Tortilla Casserole

FROM THE KITCHEN OF DIANA LEPPKE

12 (6-INCH) CORN TORTILLAS
1 1/2 POUNDS HAMBURGER
1 LARGE ONION, CHOPPED
1 (10-OUNCE) CAN ENCHILADA SAUCE
1 (4-OUNCE) CAN CHOPPED GREEN CHILES
1 (16-OUNCE) CAN CREAM OF CHICKEN SOUP
1 (16-OUNCE) CAN CREAM OF MUSHROOM SOUP
1 CUP SOUR CREAM
1 POUND MONTEREY JACK CHEESE, SHREDDED

Preheat the oven to 350° F. Cut the tortillas in small pieces. Put half
in a **9X13-INCH** buttered **CASSEROLE DISH**. In a **MEDIUM SKILLET**,
brown the beef and onion. Drain well and set aside.

In **LARGE BOWL**, mix the enchilada sauce, chiles, soups, and sour
cream. Add the meat mixture and mix thoroughly. Pour half of the
meat mixture over the tortillas. Sprinkle with half of the cheese.
Repeat the same process for the second layer. Bake for 45 minutes.
Allow to cool slightly and serve warm.

Ratatouille

FROM THE KITCHEN OF MARILYN SEUMPTEWA

2 MEDIUM TOMATOES, CUT IN WEDGES
1/8 TEASPOON THYME
1 MEDIUM ONION, SLICED
1 GREEN PEPPER, CUT IN STRIPS
2 CUPS EGGPLANT, PEELED, SLICED, AND CUT IN STRIPS
2 CUPS ZUCCHINI, SLICED AND CUT IN STRIPS
2 CLOVES GARLIC, CRUSHED
1 BAY LEAF
BLACK PEPPER, TO TASTE
1/4 CUP PARMESAN CHEESE, GRATED

Preheat the oven to 350° F. Sprinkle the tomatoes with thyme and
let stand. Sauté the remaining vegetables and garlic until barely tender. Add the bay leaf. Pour the vegetable mixture into a **1-QUART
NONSTICK CASSEROLE DISH**. Arrange the tomato wedges on top.
Sprinkle with black pepper and cheese. Bake, covered, for 30 minutes. Remove the bay leaf before serving.

Alternative Vegetable Bake

FROM THE KITCHEN OF ROBIN WRIGHT

**1 (16-OUNCE) BAG BROCCOLI, CARROTS, &
CAULIFLOWER, THAWED
1 CAN CREAM OF MUSHROOM SOUP
1 CAN FRENCH ONIONS
1 CUP SWISS CHEESE, SHREDDED**

Preheat the oven to 350° F. In a **SHALLOW BAKING DISH**, mix together the vegetables, soup, half of the French onions, and half the cheese. Bake for 30 minutes, covered. Take off the cover, sprinkle the top with the remaining onions and cheese, and bake for 5 minutes more, or until lightly brown on top. Serve warm.

Vegetable Casserole

FROM THE KITCHEN OF MARILYN SEUMPTEWA

**3 MEDIUM TOMATOES
2 POUNDS ZUCCHINI
3 MEDIUM GREEN PEPPERS
3/4 CUP GREEN ONIONS, SLICED
1/2 CUP CELERY, DICED
2 CUPS FRESH MUSHROOMS, SLICED
1/2 TEASPOON DRIED TARRAGON
1/8 TEASPOON BLACK PEPPER
1 CUP BROWN RICE, COOKED
2 OUNCES SWISS CHEESE, SHREDDED
1 1/2 CUPS CHICKEN STOCK**

Preheat the oven to 375° F. Cut the tomatoes in half and scoop out the seeds and pulp, leaving nicely walled shells. Put the pulp into a **LARGE SKILLET**. Cut the zucchini in half lengthwise and scrape out the centers leaving "canoes." Mix the zucchini pulp and the tomato pulp in the skillet.

Slice the green peppers in half lengthwise and discard the seeds. Arrange the tomato, zucchini, and green pepper halves in 2 **9X13-INCH PANS**. Set aside.

Sauté the green onions, celery, and mushrooms until wilted. Add to the zucchini and tomato pulp mixture. Mix in the tarragon, black pepper, and rice. Let cool to just warm and stir in the shredded cheese. Spoon this stuffing into the vegetable shells. Pour 3/4 cup of chicken stock into the bottom of each pan. Bake 45-60 minutes. Serve hot.

Simple Sides

The side dishes and bountiful breads you will find in this chapter have been lovingly passed down through generations with pride and care. Sample these delicious offerings from kitchens all across America's Main Street.

EXECUTIVE POTATOES

GREEN RICE

CARROTS WITH TOASTED CUMIN

ZESTY ZUCCHINI SKILLET

ASPARAGUS WITH A TWIST

APPLESAUCE

CRANBERRY DELIGHT

AMBROSIA

BANANA NUT BREAD

CHOCOLATE CHIP BANANA BREAD

RUSTIC ROUND HERB BREAD

QUICK AND EASY CORN BREAD

Executive Potatoes

FROM THE KITCHEN OF ROBIN WRIGHT

1/2 CUP BUTTER
1 (16-OUNCE) CAN CREAM OF CHICKEN SOUP
1 PINT SOUR CREAM
1 BUNCH GREEN ONIONS, CHOPPED
1 1/2 CUPS CHEDDAR CHEESE, SHREDDED
8 MEDIUM POTATOES, PEELED, COOKED, AND CHOPPED

Preheat the oven to 350° F. In a **LARGE SAUCEPAN**, melt the butter.
Add the cream of chicken soup, sour cream, green onions, and
Cheddar cheese. Mix in the chopped potatoes. Pour the mixture into
a **9X13-INCH PAN**. Bake for approximately 1 hour, or until the mixture
is golden brown and bubbly. Remove from the oven, allow to cool
slightly, and serve warm.

Green Rice

FROM THE KITCHEN OF MARILYN SEUMPTEWA

1 CUP GREEN ONIONS, CHOPPED
1 CUP FRESH PARSLEY, MINCED
4 1/2 TEASPOONS OLIVE OIL
4 1/2 TEASPOONS BUTTER
1 1/2 CUPS UNCOOKED LONG GRAIN RICE
3 CUPS CHICKEN BROTH
1/8 TEASPOON CAYENNE
1 BAY LEAF

In a medium **SAUCEPAN**, sauté the onions and parsley in the oil and
butter for 1 minute, or until tender. Add the rice and cook over
medium heat until rice is coated with oil and translucent, about 3 minutes. Stir in the broth, cayenne, and bay leaf. Bring to a boil. Reduce
the heat, cover tightly, and simmer for 18-20 minutes, or until the liquid
is absorbed and the rice is tender. Remove and discard the bay leaf.
Serve with your favorite grilled chicken or pork recipe.

Carrots with Toasted Cumin

FROM THE KITCHEN OF THERESA HOWELL

7 LARGE CARROTS, PEELED AND SLICED DIAGONALLY
3 CLOVES GARLIC, CRUSHED
2 TEASPOONS CUMIN SEEDS, TOASTED
1 TABLESPOON HONEY
1 TABLESPOON OLIVE OIL
SALT, TO TASTE
CAYENNE, TO TASTE
¼ CUP CHICKEN STOCK
LIME JUICE

Combine all ingredients except for the lime juice in a **SLOW COOKER**. Cover and cook on low for 4-6 hours. Fifteen minutes before serving, remove the lid and turn the heat to high so that remaining liquid evaporates. Immediately before serving, sprinkle with lime juice. This is a great side to serve with pork or chicken.

Zesty Zucchini Skillet

FROM THE KITCHEN OF LYDIA MCKERCHIE

1 TEASPOON OLIVE OIL
1 MEDIUM ZUCCHINI, HALVED AND SLICED
¼ CUP WHITE ONION, DICED
1 CLOVE GARLIC, CRUSHED
1 MEDIUM TOMATO, DICED
SALT, TO TASTE
BLACK PEPPER, TO TASTE
½ CUP CHEDDAR CHEESE, SHREDDED (OPTIONAL)

Pour the olive oil into a **SKILLET** over medium heat. Add the zucchini, onion, and garlic. Sauté until the onion is soft, about 3-4 minutes. Add the tomato, salt, and pepper and continue to cook until juices run. Serve topped with cheese, if desired.

Asparagus With a Twist

FROM THE KITCHEN OF LYDIA McKERCHIE

1 BUNCH ASPARAGUS
¼ TEASPOON SALT
5 TABLESPOONS BUTTER
2 TABLESPOONS LEMON JUICE
FRESHLY GROUND BLACK PEPPER, TO TASTE

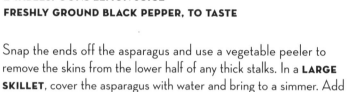

Snap the ends off the asparagus and use a vegetable peeler to remove the skins from the lower half of any thick stalks. In a **LARGE SKILLET**, cover the asparagus with water and bring to a simmer. Add the salt and cook for 5-7 minutes, or until the stalks are tender when pierced with a knife.

    Meanwhile, melt the butter in a **SMALL SAUCEPAN** and add the lemon juice and pepper. Remove the asparagus from the water and place on a **WARM SERVING PLATTER**. Pour the butter and lemon juice over the asparagus and serve.

Applesauce

FROM THE KITCHEN OF CATHY LEWIS

8-10 PIPPIN GREEN APPLES, PEELED, CORED, AND
   CUT INTO APPROXIMATELY 8 SLICES
1 ½ CUPS WATER
1 CUP SUGAR
1 TEASPOON CINNAMON
1 TEASPOON NUTMEG
2 TABLESPOONS LEMON JUICE

Place the apples in a **LARGE PAN** with the water. Cover and bring to a boil. Simmer until the apples are mushy. Mash them and add the sugar, cinnamon, nutmeg, and lemon juice. Cook for 2-3 minutes more. Spoon the applesauce into a **DECORATIVE SERVING BOWL**, and serve warm or refrigerate until cool. This sweet side dish is great served in the fall with other warm flavors of the season.

Cranberry Delight

FROM THE KITCHEN OF NANCY JENNINGS

1 BAG FRESH CRANBERRIES
1 CUP SUGAR
1 CUP PECANS, COARSELY CHOPPED
2 ORANGES, PEELED AND BROKEN INTO SECTIONS
2 APPLES, CORED AND COARSELY CHOPPED

Sort through the cranberries and remove the soft ones. Put all of the ingredients in a **FOOD PROCESSOR** and process until mixed, but not smooth. This delicious dish goes great with goat cheese and crackers or when served as an accompaniment to turkey.

Ambrosia: food of the gods

FROM THE KITCHEN OF MARK AND LAURIE WALSH

2 RED APPLES
2 BANANAS
1 (30-OUNCE) CAN FRUIT COCKTAIL, DRAINED
1 (11-OUNCE) CAN MANDARIN ORANGES, DRAINED
1 (9-OUNCE) JAR MARASCHINO CHERRIES, DRAINED
3/4 CUP COCONUT
8 OUNCES COOL WHIP
3 CUPS SMALL MARSHMALLOWS

Cut the apples and bananas into bite-size pieces. Mix all of the fruit in a **LARGE BOWL**. Mix in the coconut and cool whip. The marshmallows can be mixed in or layered on top. Serve immediately.

Banana Nut Bread

The Tee Pee, MIKE AND BETTY CALLENS
924 E. Tucumcari Blvd., Tucumcari, NM 88401, (505) 461-3773, callens@plateautel.net

1 ¹/2 CUPS SUGAR
¹/2 CUP SHORTENING
2 EGGS
4 TABLESPOONS MILK
¹/2 TEASPOON VINEGAR
2 ¹/2 CUPS FLOUR
1 TEASPOON BAKING SODA
1 TEASPOON VANILLA
2-3 RIPE BANANAS, MASHED
1 CUP WALNUTS, CHOPPED

Preheat the oven to 350° F. In a **LARGE BOWL**, combine all of the ingredients. Mix well. Pour the mixture into a greased **ANGEL FOOD CAKE PAN**, and bake for 50 minutes, or until a toothpick inserted in the center comes out clean. Allow to cool for approximately 10 minutes. Serve warm.

The Last of the Old Route 66 Curio Shops!

Tucumcari, New Mexico, at an altitude of 4,087 feet, is home of the Tee Pee Curio Store with "Damn fine stuff!" Built in the early 1940s when Route 66 was only two lanes, the Tee Pee started selling Gulf gas and groceries with a sideline of curios. As 66 grew, the store lost its gas pumps to the widening road. In its heyday, it was but one of the many curio stores bidding for business from the thousands of cars that passed by daily. But in 1981, Tucumcari was bypassed by I-40, and it spelled the end of an era. Now the Tee Pee is known for being the last of the old Route 66 curio shops, and not only in Tucumcari, but in all of eastern New Mexico.

Chocolate Chip Banana Bread

FROM THE KITCHEN OF LINDA KRANZ

1/4 CUP BUTTER OR MARGARINE, SOFTENED
3/4 CUP SUGAR
1/2 CUP SOUR CREAM
1 CUP BANANAS, MASHED
1/2 CUP SLICED ALMONDS OR WALNUTS
2 1/4 CUPS ALL-PURPOSE FLOUR
3/4 TEASPOON BAKING SODA
2 EGGS
1 TEASPOON VANILLA
1/2 CUP CHOCOLATE CHIPS
NONSTICK COOKING SPRAY

OPTIONAL:
1 TEASPOON CINNAMON
1/2 CUP CRANBERRIES

Cream the butter with the sugar. Add in the sour cream. Add the mashed bananas and nuts. Add the remaining ingredients, including the optional ingredients if desired, and blend well.

Preheat the oven to 350° F. Spray a **BREAD PAN** with nonstick cooking spray, add a little flour, and pour the bread mixture into the pan. Bake for 1 hour. Remove from the oven and allow the bread to cool slightly. Slice and serve or wrap individually for a quick snack.

Rustic Round Herb Bread

FROM THE KITCHEN OF CATHY LEWIS

2 CUPS ALL-PURPOSE FLOUR
1 CUP REDUCED-FAT CHEDDAR CHEESE, SHREDDED
1 TABLESPOON SUGAR
2 TEASPOONS BAKING POWDER
1/2 TEASPOON BAKING SODA
1/2 TEASPOON SALT
1/2 TEASPOON SAGE
1/2 TEASPOON DRIED THYME
1/2 TEASPOON DILL
3 TABLESPOONS BUTTER
1 EGG
1/2 CUP FAT-FREE PLAIN YOGURT
1/2 CUP FAT-FREE MILK
1/2 TEASPOON POPPY SEEDS

Preheat the oven to 400° F. In a **LARGE BOWL**, combine the flour, cheese, sugar, baking powder, baking soda, salt, sage, thyme, and dill. Mix well. Cut in the butter until mixture resembles fine crumbs.

In **ANOTHER BOWL**, whisk together the egg, yogurt, and milk. Stir into the dry ingredients until just moistened. Spoon into a **9-INCH ROUND BAKING PAN** coated with nonstick cooking spray. Sprinkle with the poppy seeds. Bake for 20-25 minutes, or until golden brown. Cool in the pan on a **WIRE RACK**. When ready to serve cut into wedges and place on **DECORATIVE SERVING PLATES**.

Quick & Easy Corn Bread

FROM THE KITCHEN OF LINDA KRANZ

NONSTICK COOKING SPRAY
1 (8-OUNCE) CONTAINER SOUR CREAM
1 BOX JIFFY CORN BREAD MIX
1 STICK BUTTER
1 (16-OUNCE) CAN CREAM CORN
1/2 CUP CHEDDAR CHEESE, SHREDDED

Preheat the oven to 350° F. Cream together all of the ingredients except for the cheese. Spray a **BREAD PAN** with nonstick cooking spray and pour the bread mixture into the pan. Bake for 40 minutes, or until the top starts to turn golden brown. About 10 minutes before removing the bread from the oven, sprinkle the cheese on the top. Continue cooking for 10 minutes more, or until the cheese has melted. Serve warm.

Soda Fountain Fun

This chapter is brimming with delicious drinks and desserts that will take you back to the soda shop. Remember the bright red stools, the colored lights, and the melodic doo-wop of the jukebox? Whip up a few of your favorite sweets, tune into American Bandstand, and dance the night away with Dick Clark!

MAGNIFICENT BERRY MILKSHAKE

FUNKS' FAVORITE FROSTY

VERY BERRY PARFAITS

PELE'S BANANAS & ICE CREAM

COOKIES & ICE CREAM CAKE

CARAMEL CHOCOLATE SAUCE & ICE CREAM

LEMON BLUEBERRY YOGURT DREAM

CHOCOLATE CHIP COOKIES

OATMEAL CARMELITAS

FUNKY PURE MAPLE "SIRUP" COOKIES

SPICE BARS

RHUBARB CRUNCH

CHOCOLATE ZUCCHINI CAKE

HAWAIIAN CAKE

ORANGE-RAISIN CAKE

HOT MILK CAKE

PISTACHIO BUNDT CAKE

WINE CAKE

CHOCOLATE CHEESECAKE

CREAMY CHEESECAKE

MINIATURE CHEESECAKES

JELLO CHEESECAKE

LILA'S LEMON PIE

OLGA'S CHOCOLATE PIE

APPLE CRANBERRY PIE

PRALINE & PEACH PIE

KEY LIME PIE

CREAM CHEESE PIE

Magnificent Berry Milkshake

FROM THE KITCHEN OF LYDIA MCKERCHIE

1 CUP MILK
2 CUPS FROZEN STRAWBERRIES
1 CUP FROZEN BLACKBERRIES
3 SCOOPS VANILLA ICE CREAM
WHIP CREAM AND CHERRIES (OPTIONAL)

Blend the milk, strawberries, and blackberries in the **BLENDER** until mostly smooth. Add the ice cream and blend until well mixed. Do not over blend, as the ice cream will melt. Serve in **TALL GLASSES** topped with whip cream and cherries. Enjoy!

Funks' Favorite Frosty

DEBBY FUNK, Funks Grove Pure Maple Sirup
Funks Grove, Illinois, (309) 874-3360, www.route66.com/FunksGrove

1 GLASS ICE
1 GLASS MILK
¼ CUP FUNK'S GROVE PURE MAPLE "SIRUP"

Blend all of the ingredients in a **BLENDER**, pour into a **TALL GLASS**, and enjoy!

John Weiss, author of "Traveling the New, Historic Route 66 of Illinois," created this recipe. John says that this is his favorite, most refreshing drink for a hot summer day. If you use skim milk, it is not only healthy, but also fat-free!

Very Berry Parfaits

FROM THE KITCHEN OF CATHY LEWIS

1 PACKAGE SUGAR-FREE STRAWBERRY GELATIN
1 CUP BOILING WATER
1 CUP COLD WATER
2 CUPS BLUEBERRIES
2 CUPS STRAWBERRIES, SLICED
1 3/4 CUPS FAT-FREE MILK, COLD
1 (1-OUNCE) PACKAGE SUGAR-FREE INSTANT
VANILLA PUDDING MIX

In a **BOWL**, dissolve the gelatin in boiling water. Stir in the cold water. Slowly pour into eight **PARFAIT GLASSES** and refrigerate until firm, about 1 hour.

Top with half of the blueberries and half of the strawberries. In a **BOWL**, whisk the milk and pudding mix for 2 minutes, or until slightly thickened. Pour over the berries. Top with the remaining berries. Cover and refrigerate for 1 hour longer, or until set. Serve chilled.

Pele's Bananas & Ice Cream

FROM THE KITCHEN OF NESSA SHUE

4 TABLESPOONS BUTTER
6 TABLESPOONS BROWN SUGAR
1 TEASPOON CINNAMON
4 BANANAS, SLICED LENGTHWISE
1/2 CUP BANANA LIQUEUR
1/2 CUP RUM
4 SCOOPS VANILLA ICE CREAM

Melt the butter over low heat in a **FLAMBÉ PAN** or **LARGE SKILLET**. Add the brown sugar and cinnamon and mix well. Sauté the bananas until they begin to turn soft. Add the banana liqueur and half of the rum and simmer. In a **SEPARATE SAUCEPAN**, bring the remainder of the rum to a boil. Quickly pour into the flambé pan and ignite. Allow the flame to die. In 4 **INDIVIDUAL SERVING BOWLS**, place one scoop of ice cream and top with two slices of banana. Pour the remaining sauce over the bananas and serve.

Cookies & Ice Cream Cake

FROM THE KITCHEN OF BETTY MARCUS

2 PINTS QUALITY COFFEE ICE CREAM
20 (2-INCH DIAMETER) HOMEMADE CHOCOLATE
  CHIP COOKIES
1/2 CUP COFFEE BEAN CANDIES, CHOPPED
1 CUP WHIPPING CREAM, CHILLED
1 TABLESPOON SUGAR
1 TEASPOON KAHLUA

Soften the ice cream in the refrigerator so that it is semi-soft and workable, although not melted.

Line a **5X9-INCH LOAF PAN** with plastic wrap so that it hangs over the sides. Line the bottom with a layer of chocolate chip cookies placed flat-side down. If the cookies don't cover completely, break a few apart and fill in the gaps. Cover the cookie layer with 1 pint of the softened ice cream, packing down with a spoon. Sprinkle the ice cream with 1/3 of the chopped coffee bean candies. Add another layer of cookies, all crumbled this time to make a consistent layer. Spread the remaining pint of ice cream on top, making sure to pack it down well, and sprinkle with the other 1/3 of the coffee bean candies. Reserve the remaining coffee bean candies for the topping. Top it off with a final layer of whole cookies, pushing down firmly to pack the cake. Cover the cake with plastic wrap, and then add aluminum foil over the top to seal well. Freeze overnight.

About 1 hour before serving the cake, fill the sink with semi-hot water. Set the frozen bread pan in the hot water so that it comes most of the way up the sides of pan, but does not get into the ice cream layers. Leave the pan in the water until the ice cream releases from the pan, and quickly pull it out by the plastic wrap. Completely unwrap the loaf, turn it upside-down onto a **PLATE**, and refreeze.

After the cake has refrozen, beat the whipped cream, sugar, and Kahlua until stiff peaks form. Generously frost the cake and sprinkle with remaining coffee bean candies. Either refreeze until ready to serve or serve immediately.

Caramel Chocolate Sauce & Ice Cream

FROM THE KITCHEN OF MARILYN SEUMPTEWA

30 CARAMEL SQUARES
1 (6-OUNCE) PACKAGE SEMI-SWEET CHOCOLATE CHIPS
1 (5-OUNCE) CAN EVAPORATED MILK
1/2 CUP BUTTER (NO SUBSTITUTES)
ICE CREAM

In a **1-QUART MICROWAVE-SAFE BOWL**, combine the caramels, chocolate chips, milk, and butter. Microwave uncovered for 2 minutes, and then mix well. Microwave again for 1-2 minutes more, or until the caramels are almost melted. Stir until smooth. Serve warm over your favorite flavor of ice cream.

Lemon Blueberry Yogurt Dream

FROM THE KITCHEN OF MARILYN SEUMPTEWA

1 (8-OUNCE) CARTON FROZEN WHIPPED TOPPING, THAWED
1 CUP FRESH BLUEBERRIES
1 (8-OUNCE) CARTON LEMON YOGURT

Fold the whipped topping and blueberries into the yogurt. Spoon into **INDIVIDUAL SERVING BOWLS** and serve immediately.

Chocolate Chip Cookies

FROM THE KITCHEN OF MARILYN SEUMPTEWA

1 CUP SUGAR
1 CUP BROWN SUGAR
1 CUP BUTTER, SOFTENED
2 EGGS
1 1/2 TEASPOONS VANILLA
3 CUPS ALL-PURPOSE FLOUR
1 TEASPOON SALT
1 TEASPOON BAKING SODA
1 (12-OUNCE) PACKAGE SEMI-SWEET CHOCOLATE CHIPS

Preheat the oven to 375° F. In a **LARGE BOWL**, mix together the sugar, brown sugar, and butter. Mix in the eggs and vanilla. In a separate **SMALL BOWL**, sift the flour, salt, and baking soda together. Gradually add the flour mixture to the sugar mixture. Stir in the chocolate chips. Drop by teaspoonfuls onto a greased baking sheet, approximately 2 inches apart, and bake for 10-12 minutes, or until golden brown.

Oatmeal Carmelitas

FROM THE KITCHEN OF DIANA LEPPKE

50 CARAMEL SQUARES
1/2 CUP EVAPORATED MILK
2 CUPS FLOUR
2 CUPS QUICK OATS
1 1/2 CUPS PACKED BROWN SUGAR
1 TEASPOON SODA
1/2 TEASPOON SALT
1 CUP BUTTER OR MARGARINE, MELTED
2 CUPS CHOCOLATE CHIPS
1 CUP WALNUTS, CHOPPED

In a **MEDIUM SAUCEPAN**, melt the caramels with the milk. Remove from heat and allow to cool slightly.

Preheat the oven to 350° F. In a **MEDIUM BOWL**, combine the flour, oats, sugar, soda, and salt. Mix well. Add the melted butter and press half of the mixture in a **9X13-INCH PAN**. Bake for 10 minutes. After 10 minutes, sprinkle the oat mixture with chocolate chips and nuts, and then drizzle the melted caramel over the top. Cover with the remaining half of oatmeal mixture, pressing down slightly. Bake for 15 to 20 minutes longer. Cool in the pan and cut into bars.

Funky Pure Maple "Sirup" Cookies

VAL FUNK, Funks Grove Pure Maple Sirup
Funks Grove, Illinois, (309) 874-3360, www.route66.com/FunksGrove

1 1/3 CUPS BUTTER, MELTED
2 CUPS SUGAR
2 LARGE EGGS, BEATEN
1/2 CUP PURE FUNKS MAPLE "SIRUP"
4 TEASPOONS BAKING SODA
1 TEASPOON SALT
1 TEASPOON VANILLA
4 CUPS UNSIFTED FLOUR
1/2 CUP WHITE SUGAR

Mix the melted butter with the sugar. Let cool and add the beaten eggs. Add the maple sirup, soda, salt, and vanilla. Add the flour and mix thoroughly. Chill the dough overnight in the refrigerator or for a couple of hours.

When ready to bake, preheat the oven to 350° F. Roll the dough into walnut size balls, roll them in the sugar, and place them on a greased **COOKIE SHEET**. Flatten them with a spatula. Put the oven rack into the middle position. Bake the cookies for 10-12 minutes, or until lightly browned. Remove from the oven and after 1 minute, move the cookies to a **WIRE RACK** to let cool.

Note: These cookies are easy and make quite a few. They are fast rivaling Grandma Funk's sugar cookies, and trust me, that's hard to do! As for the brand, I'm sure any real maple "sirup" will work, but being from the Funk family, I obviously have a fondness for this brand.

A word of advice—spray the inside of your measuring cup with cooking spray before pouring in the sirup. It will keep the sirup from sticking to the cup. It really works! ENJOY!

Spice Bars

FROM THE KITCHEN OF DORIS CAVIS

BARS:
1 CUP SEEDLESS RAISINS
1 CUP WATER
1/2 CUP SALAD OIL
1 CUP WHITE SUGAR
1 EGG, LIGHTLY BEATEN
1 3/4 CUPS ALL-PURPOSE FLOUR
1/4 TEASPOON SALT
1 TEASPOON BAKING SODA
1 TEASPOON CINNAMON
1 TEASPOON NUTMEG
1 TEASPOON ALL SPICE
1/2 TEASPOON CLOVES
1/2 CUP NUTS, CHOPPED
1 CUP CHOCOLATE CHIPS

FROSTING:
1/4 CUP BUTTER
1 CUP CONFECTIONER'S SUGAR

Preheat the oven to 350° F. Put the raisins in water and bring to a boil. Remove from the heat and stir in the oil. Cool slightly. Stir in the sugar and egg, and add the remaining dry ingredients, except for the nuts and chocolate chips. Beat into the raisin mixture. Stir in the nuts and chocolate chips. Pour into a **9X13-INCH GREASED PAN**. Bake for 20-25 minutes, or until golden brown on top.

In a **SEPARATE BOWL**, mix the frosting ingredients. If it is too thick, add a little cream or milk until you reach the desired consistency. Spread generously on the cooled bars and serve immediately.

Rhubarb Crunch

FROM THE KITCHEN OF LINDA STEIN JEROME

1 CUP ALL-PURPOSE FLOUR
3/4 CUP UNCOOKED OATMEAL
1 CUP BROWN SUGAR
1/2 CUP BUTTER, MELTED
1 TEASPOON CINNAMON
4 CUPS RHUBARB, DICED (FRESH OR FROZEN)
1 CUP SUGAR
2 TABLESPOONS CORNSTARCH
1 CUP WATER
1 TEASPOON VANILLA

Preheat the oven to 350° F. In a **MEDIUM BOWL**, mix the flour, oatmeal, brown sugar, butter, and cinnamon until crumbly. Press half the mixture into a greased **9-INCH BAKING DISH**. Cover with the diced rhubarb.

In a **SEPARATE BOWL**, combine the sugar, cornstarch, water, and vanilla. Mix until it is thick and clear. Pour over the rhubarb in the baking dish. Top with the remaining oatmeal mixture and bake for 1 hour. Serve warm topped with whipped cream or ice cream.

Chocolate Zucchini Cake

FROM THE KITCHEN OF DIANE CAVIS

1/2 CUP BUTTER OR MARGARINE
2 EGGS
1/4 CUP OIL
1/2 CUP SOUR MILK
1 3/4 CUPS SUGAR
1/2 TEASPOON SALT
1 TEASPOON VANILLA
4 TABLESPOONS COCOA POWDER
1 TEASPOON BAKING SODA
1/2 TEASPOON BAKING POWDER
2 1/2 CUPS FLOUR
3/4 TEASPOON CINNAMON
1/2 TEASPOON CLOVES
2 CUPS ZUCCHINI, GRATED

Preheat the oven to 325° F. Grease and flour a **9X13-INCH PAN**.
Cream together the butter, eggs, oil, milk, sugar, salt, and vanilla. In a
SEPARATE BOWL, stir together the remaining dry ingredients. Add to
liquid mixture. Mix well. Pour into the pan and bake for 40-45 minutes. Allow to cool slightly and serve warm.

Hawaiian Cake

THE ADAM FAMILY, The Ariston Café
South Old Route 66, Litchfield, IL 62056, (217) 324-2023, www.ariston-cafe.com

CAKE:
2 CUPS ALL-PURPOSE FLOUR
2 CUPS SUGAR
2 EGGS, BEATEN
1 TABLESPOON BAKING SODA
1 CUP COCONUT
1/2 CUP NUTS, CRUSHED
1 (20-OUNCE) CAN CRUSHED PINEAPPLE
   WITH LIQUID

FROSTING:
4 OUNCES CREAM CHEESE
1 STICK BUTTER, SOFTENED
1 CUP POWDERED SUGAR
1 TEASPOON VANILLA
4 OUNCES COOL WHIP

Preheat the oven to 350° F. Place all of the ingredients in a **LARGE BOWL** and stir by hand. Mix well. Grease a **9X13-INCH PAN**. Pour the cake batter into the pan and bake for 40 minutes, or until golden brown and set in the center.

    To make the frosting, beat all of the frosting ingredients in a **MEDIUM BOWL**. Generously spread on the cooled cake and serve immediately.

Orange-Raisin Cake

FROM THE KITCHEN OF DIANA LEPPKE

CAKE:
1 ORANGE, SEPARATED INTO PIECES
1 CUP RAISINS
1/2 CUP SHORTENING
1 CUP SUGAR
2 EGGS
2 CUPS ALL-PURPOSE FLOUR
1 TEASPOON SODA
1 TEASPOON BAKING POWDER
1/2 TEASPOON SALT
1 CUP BUTTERMILK
1 TEASPOON VANILLA

GLAZE:
JUICE OF 1 ORANGE
1/2 CUP SUGAR

FROSTING:
3 OUNCES CREAM CHEESE
3 TABLESPOONS MARGARINE OR BUTTER, MELTED
2 CUPS POWDERED SUGAR
1/4 CUP RESERVED ORANGE RAISIN MIX

Preheat the oven to 350° F. In a **SMALL BOWL**, mix together the orange pieces and the raisins. Set aside. In a **SEPARATE BOWL**, cream together the shortening and the sugar. Add the eggs and mix well.

In a **MEDIUM BOWL**, mix the flour, soda, baking powder, and the salt. Add the buttermilk and the flour mixture to the egg mixture. Add the vanilla and 3/4 cup of the orange raisin mixture. Set aside the remaining 1/4 cup for the frosting. Pour the cake batter into a greased **9X13-INCH BAKING PAN**, and bake for 25 minutes, or until a knife inserted in the center comes out clean.

Meanwhile, mix the glaze ingredients. Remove the cake from the oven and poke holes in it with a toothpick. Spoon the glaze over the cake while it is still warm. Let cool.

To make the frosting, mix all of the frosting ingredients and generously spread over the cooled cake. Serve immediately.

Hot Milk Cake

FROM THE KITCHEN OF DORIS CAVIS

CAKE:
2 EGGS
1 CUP SUGAR
1 TEASPOON VANILLA
1 CUP ALL-PURPOSE FLOUR
1 TEASPOON BAKING POWDER
1/2 CUP MILK, WARMED
2 TABLESPOONS BUTTER, MELTED

ICING:
3 TABLESPOONS BUTTER, MELTED
2 TABLESPOONS MILK
5 TABLESPOONS BROWN SUGAR
1/2 CUP COCONUT

Preheat the oven to 350° F. Beat the eggs for 3 minutes. Add the sugar and beat well. Add the vanilla, flour, and baking powder. Add the warm milk and melted butter. Beat well and pour into a buttered **SQUARE PAN**. Bake for 40 minutes, or until a knife inserted in the center comes out clean.

In a **SEPARATE BOWL**, mix all of the icing ingredients, and spread on top of the cake while warm. Place the frosted cake very low under the broiler. Broil until it lightly bubbles. Watch it, as it will burn quickly. Remove and serve warm.

Pistachio Bundt Cake

FROM THE KITCHEN OF MARY GALES

1 PACKAGE YELLOW CAKE MIX
1 CUP ORANGE JUICE
1 BOX PISTACHIO PUDDING MIX
4 EGGS
1/2 CUP COOKING OIL
1/4 CUP CRÈME DE MENTHE
3/4 CUP CHOCOLATE SYRUP
1 CONTAINER CHOCOLATE FROSTING

Preheat the oven to 350° F. In a **MEDIUM BOWL**, mix all of the ingredients except for the chocolate syrup and the frosting. Pour 2/3 of the batter into a greased and floured **BUNDT PAN**. To the remaining 1/3 batter, add the chocolate syrup. Pour over the first mixture and marbleize by pulling a knife through the batter. Bake for approximately 1 hour, or until a knife inserted in the center comes out clean.

Remove the cake from the oven and allow to cool slightly. Frost with your favorite chocolate frosting, and serve immediately.

Wine Cake

FROM THE KITCHEN OF DIANA LEPPKE

1 PACKAGE YELLOW CAKE MIX
1 PACKAGE VANILLA INSTANT PUDDING
6 EGGS
3/4 CUP OIL
1 CUP SHERRY
2 TEASPOONS NUTMEG
1/2 CUP NUTS, FINELY CHOPPED
1/2 CUP POWDERED SUGAR

Preheat the oven to 350° F. In a **MEDIUM BOWL**, mix all of the ingredients together except for the powdered sugar. Pour into a greased **BUNDT PAN**, and bake for 45 minutes. Allow to cool for 5 minutes before removing the cake from the pan. While still warm, sprinkle the top with the powdered sugar. This cake tastes like a rich, brandied eggnog and is elegant enough to serve for company.

Chocolate Cheesecake

FROM THE KITCHEN OF NESSA SHUE

CRUST:
3/4 CUP GRAHAM CRACKER CRUMBS,
    APPROXIMATELY 5 CRACKERS
5 TABLESPOONS BUTTER, MELTED
2 TABLESPOONS SUGAR
2 TABLESPOONS SEMI-SWEET CHOCOLATE, GRATED

FILLING:
3 EGGS
1 CUP SUGAR
24 OUNCES CREAM CHEESE, SOFTENED
1 (12-OUNCE) PACKAGE SEMI-SWEET
    CHOCOLATE CHIPS
1 CUP SOUR CREAM
3/4 CUP BUTTER
1 TEASPOON VANILLA
1 CUP PECANS, CHOPPED
WHIPPED CREAM

Combine all of the crust ingredients and press firmly into the bottom of a **9-INCH FORM PAN**. Chill in the refrigerator.

Preheat oven to 325° F. To make the filling, combine the eggs and sugar and blend until light and creamy. Add the softened cream cheese, blending until well mixed. In a **DOUBLE BROILER**, combine the chocolate, sour cream, butter, and vanilla. Simmer until the chocolate is melted. Stir the chocolate mixture into the cream cheese mixture. Fold in the pecans. Pour into the spring form pan on top of the crust and bake for 2 hours, or until the center is firm. Let the cake cool on a **WIRE RACK**. Chill for approximately 12 hours and serve with whipped cream on top.

Creamy Cheesecake

FROM THE KITCHEN OF MOLLY OPHOVEN

1 1/2 CUPS CRUSHED OREOS, APPROXIMATELY 18 COOKIES
1/2 CUP BUTTER, MELTED
3 (8-OUNCE) PACKAGES CREAM CHEESE, SOFTENED
1 (14-OUNCE) CAN SWEETENED CONDENSED MILK
3 EGGS
2 TEASPOONS VANILLA
1 CUP SEMI-SWEET MINI CHOCOLATE CHIPS
1 TEASPOON ALL-PURPOSE FLOUR

Preheat the oven to 300° F. In a **SMALL BOWL**, combine the crushed Oreos and butter. Pat on the bottom of a **SPRING FORM PAN**.

In a **SEPARATE BOWL**, beat the cream cheese until fluffy. Add the sweetened milk and beat until smooth. Add the eggs and vanilla. Mix well.

In **SMALL BOWL**, toss together 1/2 cup of the chocolate chips with flour to coat. Stir into the cream cheese mixture and pour into the prepared pan over the Oreo crust. Sprinkle rest of the chips over the top. Bake for 1 hour, or until the cake springs back. Serve immediately.

Miniature Cheesecakes

FROM THE KITCHEN OF MARILYN SEUMPTEWA

24 VANILLA WAFERS
2 (8-OUNCE) PACKAGES CREAM CHEESE
3/4 CUP SUGAR
1 TABLESPOON FRESH LEMON JUICE
1 TEASPOON VANILLA
2 EGGS
1 CAN FRUIT PIE FILLING
1/2 CUP SLICED NUTS (OPTIONAL)

Preheat the oven to 375° F. Separate 24 cupcake liners and place the liners in **CUPCAKE PANS**. Place a vanilla wafer in the bottom of each liner.

In a **SMALL BOWL**, beat the cream cheese, sugar, lemon juice, vanilla, and eggs until light and fluffy. Fill the liners 2/3-full with the cream cheese mixture. Bake for 15-20 minutes, or until set. Top each cheesecake with a spoonful of fruit pie filling and a few sliced nuts, if desired. Chill and serve cold.

Jello Cheesecake

FROM THE KITCHEN OF MARY GALES

CRUST:
30 GRAHAM CRACKERS, CRUSHED
1 TEASPOON SUGAR
1 STICK BUTTER OR MARGARINE, MELTED

FILLING:
1 (11-OUNCE) CAN EVAPORATED MILK
1 PACKAGE LEMON JELLO
1 CUP WATER, BOILING
1 CUP SUGAR
2 (3-OUNCE) PACKAGES CREAM CHEESE
1 TEASPOON VANILLA

In a **MEDIUM BOWL**, mix the crackers, sugar, and melted butter. Remove approximately 1/2 and reserve for the topping. Pat the remaining cracker mixture into the bottom of a **9X13-INCH CAKE PAN** and chill.

Thoroughly chill a **LARGE MIXING BOWL** and the can of evaporated milk. In a **SEPARATE BOWL**, mix the lemon Jello and boiling water. Cool slightly, but do not set. Add the sugar, cream cheese, and vanilla. Set aside.

In the chilled bowl, whip the evaporated milk. Fold the Jello mixture into milk and mix carefully until smooth. Spread on the chilled crust. Sprinkle the reserved cracker mixture on top. Let set in the refrigerator for about 4 hours. Serve chilled.

Lila's Lemon Pie

Jude Leonard, Miz Zip's Café
2924 East Route 66, Flagstaff, AZ 86004, (928) 526-0104

PIE:
2 1/2 CUPS SUGAR
2/3 CUP CORNSTARCH
1/2 TEASPOON SALT
3 1/2 CUPS WATER
4 LARGE EGG YOLKS, BEATEN (RESERVE THE
WHITES FOR THE MERINGUE)
1/4 CUP LEMON ZEST, ABOUT 3 LEMONS
1/2 - 1 CUP LEMON JUICE, ABOUT 4 LEMONS
2 (9-INCH) PRE-BAKED PIE CRUSTS

MERINGUE:
8 EGG WHITES
8 TABLESPOONS SUGAR

In a **LARGE SAUCEPAN**, add the sugar, cornstarch, salt, and water. Cook until thick and clear. Add the beaten egg yolks to the sugar mixture and cook a few minutes more. Remove from the heat and mix in the lemon zest and juice. Pour into the pie crusts and set aside.

Preheat the oven to 350° F. In a **SEPARATE BOWL**, beat the egg whiles until frothy. Add the sugar and beat until it forms soft peaks. Top the pies with meringue and seal to the edges. Bake for 10–15 minutes, or until lightly browned on top.

L and L Motel Café was Miz Zips' predecessor. The business was acquired by Joe and Lila Lockhart at a sheriff's sale, and they successfully ran it with their son Bob Leonard and his wife Norma in the early fifties. To this day, the gas bill comes in the name of L and L Motel Café and the phone bill comes to Joe Lockhart.

This business is an original Route 66 diner that has operated as a truck stop and locals' café for many years. It is known for its good home cookin' and homey atmosphere. The locals are what make us thrive. Their favorite menu items are the chicken-fried steak, the chile, and, of course, the Zip burger.

Bob Leonard talked Craig into buying the business in 1991, wanting to keep it in the family. It is presently owned and operated by Craig and Jude Leonard (third generation), with their children, Lori and Erin (fourth generation). This past summer, grandchildren Bradley and Cassie (fifth generation), ages 14 and 10, also helped out. As we always say, "Our customers are our friends."

Olga's Chocolate Pie

JUDE LEONARD, Miz Zip's Café
2924 East Route 66, Flagstaff, AZ 86004, (928) 526-0104

PIE:
1 CUP MILK
1/3 CUP SUGAR
3 1/3 TABLESPOONS CORNSTARCH
1/3 TABLESPOON ALL-PURPOSE FLOUR
1 TEASPOON SALT
3 SQUARES UNSWEETENED CHOCOLATE
4 LARGE EGGS YOLKS, BEATEN
1 TEASPOON VANILLA
2 (9-INCH) PRE-BAKED PIE CRUSTS

MERINGUE:
4 EGG WHITES
4 TABLESPOONS SUGAR

Heat the milk in a **LARGE PAN** to scalding. In a **MEDIUM BOWL**, mix the sugar, cornstarch, flour, salt, and chocolate. Add the sugar mixture to the milk, and whisk until thick. Add the beaten egg yolks and cook for a few minutes more. Remove from the heat and whisk in the vanilla. Pour into two pre-baked pie shells.

Preheat the oven to 350° F. In a **SEPARATE BOWL**, beat the egg whites until frothy. Add the sugar and beat until it forms soft peaks. Top the pie with meringue and seal to the edges. Bake for 10-15 minutes, or until lightly browned on top.

Mary Nemire, one of our regular customers, has her weekly chocolate fix by eating a piece of this delicious pie every Wednesday, calling in the morning to make sure we save her a piece.

Apple Cranberry Pie

FROM THE KITCHEN OF MARY GALES

2 (9-INCH) UNBAKED PASTRY SHELLS

3/4 CUP BROWN SUGAR
1/4 CUP SUGAR
1/3 CUP ALL-PURPOSE FLOUR
1 TEASPOON CINNAMON
4 CUPS TART APPLES, PARED AND SLICED
2 CUPS CRANBERRIES, FRESH OR FROZEN
2 TABLESPOONS MARGARINE

Preheat the oven to 425° F. In a **LARGE BOWL**, combine the sugars, flour, and cinnamon. Add the apples and cranberries. Mix until well coated. Pour apple mixture into pastry-lined pie pan. Dot with the butter. Cover with the second pie crust and cut slits into the top crust. Seal the edges. Bake for 40 minutes, or until golden brown. Allow to cool slightly and serve warm.

Praline & Peach Pie

FROM THE KITCHEN OF DIANA LEPPKE

1 TEASPOON ALL-PURPOSE FLOUR
1 (9-INCH) UNBAKED PASTRY SHELL
1/2 CUP LIGHT CORN SYRUP
3 EGGS
1/4 CUP SUGAR
3 TABLESPOONS ALL-PURPOSE FLOUR
1/4 TEASPOON SALT
1/4 TEASPOON FRESHLY GRATED NUTMEG
3 CUPS FRESH PEACHES, PEELED AND CUBED
1/2 CUP BUTTER OR MARGARINE, MELTED
1/2 CUP PECANS, COARSELY CHOPPED
1/4 CUP ALL-PURPOSE FLOUR
1/2 CUP BROWN SUGAR, PACKED
2 TABLESPOONS BUTTER, SOFTENED
WHIPPED CREAM (OPTIONAL)
VANILLA ICE CREAM (OPTIONAL)

Preheat the oven to 350° F. Sprinkle 1 teaspoon of the flour over the unbaked pastry shell; set aside. In a **LARGE BOWL**, combine the corn syrup, eggs, 1/4 cup sugar, 3 tablespoons flour, salt, and nutmeg. Beat at medium speed for 1 minute. Stir in the peaches and 1/2 cup melted butter. Pour the peach mixture into the prepared pastry shell.

In a **MEDIUM BOWL**, combine the pecans, 1/4 cup flour, and 1/2 cup brown sugar. Mix well. Cut the 2 tablespoons of butter into the pecan mixture until it is crumbly. Sprinkle the pecan mixture evenly over the peach mixture. Bake for 45-50 minutes, or until the pie is set. Let cool completely. If desired, serve topped with whipped cream or ice cream.

Key Lime Pie

FROM THE KITCHEN OF CATHY LEWIS

FILLING:
4 TEASPOONS LIME ZEST
4 LARGE EGG YOLKS
1 (14-OUNCE) CAN SWEETENED CONDENSED MILK
1/2 CUP JUICE, ABOUT 3-4 LIMES

CRUST:
1 1/4 CUPS GRAHAM CRACKERS, PROCESSED TO FINE CRUMBS
3 TABLESPOONS GRANULATED SUGAR
5 TABLESPOONS UNSALTED BUTTER, MELTED

TOPPING:
3/4 HEAVY CREAM
1/4 CUP CONFECTIONER'S SUGAR
1/2 LIME, SLICED PAPER THIN AND DIPPED IN SUGAR (OPTIONAL)

To make the filling, whisk the zest and egg yolks in a **MEDIUM BOWL** until tinted light green, about 2 minutes. Beat in the condensed milk, and then the lime juice. Set aside at room temperature to thicken.

Move the oven rack to the center position and preheat to 325° F. To make the crust, mix the cracker crumbs and sugar in a **MEDIUM BOWL**. Add the butter, and stir with a fork until well blended. Pour the butter mixture into a **9-INCH PIE PAN**. Press the crumbs over the bottom and sides of the pan to form an even crust. Bake until lightly browned and fragrant, about 15 minutes. Transfer the pan to a **WIRE RACK** and allow the crust to cool to room temperature, about 20 minutes.

Pour the lime filling into the cooled crust. Bake until the center in set, yet wiggly when jiggled, about 15-17 minutes. Return the pie to the wire rack, and allow to cool to room temperature. Refrigerate until well chilled, at least 3 hours.

To make the topping, whip the cream in a **MEDIUM BOWL** until very soft peaks form. Add the confectioner's sugar 1 tablespoon at a time, continuing to whip to just stiff peaks. Decoratively pipe the whipped cream over the pie or spread evenly with a rubber spatula. Garnish, if desired, with sugared lime slices and serve immediately.

Cream Cheese Pie

FROM THE KITCHEN OF CATHY LEWIS

CRUST:
1 1/3 CUPS GRAHAM CRACKER CRUMBS
1/3 CUP BROWN SUGAR
1 TEASPOON CINNAMON
1/3 CUP BUTTER, MELTED

FILLING:
1 (8-OUNCE) PACKAGE CREAM CHEESE, SOFTENED
1 (15-OUNCE) CAN CONDENSED MILK
1/3 CUP LEMON JUICE
1 TEASPOON VANILLA

TOPPINGS:
CHERRY PIE FILLING
BLUEBERRY PIE FILLING
CHOCOLATE SAUCE

To make the pie crust, mix all of the crust ingredients together and gently press into a **9-INCH PIE PAN**. Chill in the refrigerator while preparing the filling.

To make the filling, beat the cream cheese until light and fluffy. Gradually add the milk until blended. Add the lemon juice and vanilla and mix well. Pour into the chilled pie crust. Refrigerate for at least 2 hours. Just before serving, generously spread the fruit filling or chocolate sauce over the top of the pie and serve immediately.